101
QUESTIONS

ABOUT
REPRODUCTION

OR HOW 1 + 1 = 3 OR
4 OR MORE . . .

101
QUESTIONS
ABOUT
REPRODUCTION

OR HOW 1 + 1 = 3
OR 4 OR MORE . . .

· · · · ·

FAITH HICKMAN BRYNIE

· · · · ·

 Twenty-First Century Books • Minneapolis

Cover Photograph courtesy of © CiCi Mann/Images.com, Inc.
Photographs courtesy of Photo Researchers, Inc.: pp. 19 (© David M. Phillips), 40 (all © Dr. Yorgos Nikas/SPL), 58 (© James Wvinner), 77 (© Saturn Stills), 126 (© Science Photo Library); Ben Osborne/University of Adelaide: p. 33; Phototake, Inc.: pp. 68 (© Steve Oh, M.S.), 120 (© Ansell Horn), 132 (© Yoav Levy); © Sabina Dowell: p. 73; Heater Advertising, Boston: p. 95; Photo Researchers, Inc./CNRI/Science Photo Library: p. 98; © Max Aguilera-Hellweg/Time Life Pictures/Getty Images: p. 151. Diagrams by Sharon Lane Holm.

Twenty First Century Books
A division of Lerner Publishing Group
241 First Avenue North
Minneapolis, Minnesota 55401 U.S.A.

Website address: www.lernerbooks.com

Library of Congress Cataloging-in-Publication Data

Brynie, Faith Hickman, 1946–
    101 questions about reproduction : or how 1 + 1 = 3 or 4 or more / Faith Brynie.
        p.   cm.
    Summary: Uses a question-and-answer format to present information about physical, medical, and social issues surrounding human reproduction, including birth control, pregnancy, and childbirth.
    Includes bibliographical references and index.
    ISBN-13: 978–0–7613-2311-2 (lib. bdg. : alk. paper)
    ISBN-10: 0–7613-2311-2 (lib. bdg. : alk. paper)
    1. Human reproduction—Juvenile literature. [1. Reproduction. 2. Sex instruction for youth. 3. Questions and answers.] I. Title: One hundred one questions about reproduction. II. Title.
QP251.5.B79 2006
612.6—dc22   2003016350

Manufactured in the United States of America
1 2 3 4 5 6 – JR – 11 10 09 08 07 06

CONTENTS

ACKNOWLEDGMENTS

The author appreciates the contributions of all those who helped make this book a reality. Jill Losee-Hoehlein, Great Bridge High School, Chesapeake, Virginia, and her school's Family Living students provided some of the questions answered in this book. Thanks to all those young people who provided the rest via the Internet. There would be no book without them.

On all matters medical, the author is grateful for guidance provided by Elizabeth Stein. She is a Certified Nurse Midwife with many years experience and a busy practice in New York City. She treats women and families all day, delivers babies all night, and still found time to answer many more than 101 of this author's questions. Thanks also to Eric Dyson, Communications Manager of the American College of Nurse Midwives, for putting us in touch.

The author is also grateful to Rebecca Flynn O'Brien, Assistant Professor of Pediatrics at Tufts University and Attending Pediatrician/Adolescent Medicine at the New England Medical Center for her thoughtful, critical review. The fascinating story of the stumpy lizard came courtesy of Suzy Munns and Chris Daniels, Department of Environmental Biology, University of Adelaide, Adelaide, Australia. Appreciation also to Jim Zhang of the National Institute of Child Health and Human Development for sharing pre-publication data on labor and delivery.

Alice Walker was right when she wrote, "My daughter's birth was the incomparable gift of seeing the world at quite a different angle than before." Thanks to Ann for the ever-changing tilt that realigns me daily. And, as always, infinite gratitude to Lloyd. He is my center and my sustenance.

FOREWORD

Reproduction. It's as basic as breathing, and equally vital. Our species would not continue without it. Yet what do we really know of it? Those mysterious processes that form sperm and egg take place hidden from view. Neither woman nor man knows when those cells unite, and months pass before the first kicks in her abdomen tell a woman her doctor isn't lying: She really is pregnant.

The processes of growth, development, and readiness for independent life happen unseen as well. Nine months of change within the womb offer few outward signs, aside from a woman's ever-expanding middle. Only at the moment of birth is the invisible revealed, and expectant parents become parents. Only then do a man and a woman see the reality of reproduction: that they have, indeed, passed to another generation the genetic material they acquired from generations before.

This book is about the unseen realities of reproduction. Some of them are, admittedly, not as joyful as the arrival of a much wanted and much loved child. Behind the scenes of healthy, happy childbearing lie many risks. Chance, bad judgment, and forces beyond human control may endanger the health of parents or the viability of their offspring. Pregnancies happen when they aren't wanted, or fail to occur when they are. Some babies are born healthy. Some are born deformed and ill. Some die. Most, however, greet life with a lusty cry and thrive through infancy and childhood. They grow into intelligent and curious young adults eager to comprehend the incomprehensible. This book is for them.

A NOTE ABOUT SEX

This book contains many questions and answers about the reproductive outcomes of sexual activity, but questions about sex and sexuality *per se* are conspicuous in their absence. They have been omitted here not because they lack importance, but because these topics have been treated in another book in this series, *101 Questions About Sex and Sexuality . . . With Answers for the Curious, Cautious, and Confused* (Twenty-First Century Books, 2003). Interested readers are encouraged to consult it for answers to questions about sexual feelings and actions, masturbation, sexual development and maturation, and sex crimes. The book also contains a chapter on the most common sexually transmitted diseases (STDs) and a detailed analysis of the question of sexual orientation. More important, it probes in detail the fundamental questions of when and why young people choose to have sex—or choose not to.

CHAPTER ONE

THAT SHOULD COME FIRST

The important thing in science is not so much to obtain new facts as to discover new ways of thinking about them.
• SIR WILLIAM BRAGG •

How Do Living Things Reproduce?

Reproduction is simply the passage of genes from one generation to the next. Genes are pieces of DNA. DNA is the master molecule that controls what goes on in living cells. It makes living things different. Oak trees, tigers, and humans are different because they have different DNA. Reproduction is the reason they survive—not as individuals, but as forms of life—over hundreds, thousands, even millions of years.

As humans, we think of reproduction as two parents, sexual inter-course, and the union of male and female sex cells inside a woman's body. During pregnancy, a fetus grows, and some nine months later, an infant is born. We see evidence of genes in the resemblance of the child to its parents.

Nature, however, has more than one way of preserving and transmitting DNA through time. Two parents aren't always necessary. Viruses, for example, reproduce asexually (without sex). They infect living cells and multiply their DNA (or, in some cases, a similar genetic molecule, RNA) using the gene-copying machinery of their host. Bacteria, yeasts, and some single-celled plants and animals also reproduce asexually, but without the need for a host. They simply make exact copies of themselves. One cell divides into two, two into four, four into eight, and so on.

Fungi and ferns have the best of both worlds. They can reproduce alone or with a partner. A single bread mold, *Rhizopus*, releases spores that grow into exact duplicates of itself. That's asexual reproduction, but *Rhizopus* can reproduce sexually too. If the hyphae (which look something like underground roots) of one *Rhizopus* grow near the hyphae of another, they fuse and combine their genetic material. From the fused hyphae grows another *Rhizopus*. Genetically, it's a combination of DNA from its two parents.

Some insects, earthworms, fish, lizards, and snakes are capable of parthenogenesis, or development from the female's unfertilized egg. This usually means that females produce exact duplicates of themselves. No male reproductive cells are needed, and no male offspring result. There are variations on this theme, however. Scientists in Colorado and Arizona found male snakes in litters produced by virgin female garter snakes and timber rattlesnakes. This happens because, through a series of unexpected steps, the egg is capable of fertilizing itself with part of the female's own genetic material.[1]

Despite these variations, the most common way to reproduce is sex, but that doesn't necessarily mean separate genders. Consider the humble tapeworm. Its body is made of segments called proglottids. Proglottids are packets of reproductive organs, both male and female. The male organs make sperm, and the female organs make eggs. When sperm and egg combine, the tapeworm has fertilized itself, making nothing more exciting than another proglottid to add to the tapeworm's ever-lengthening chain. The oldest proglottids at the end of the chain pass out through the feces of the worm's host. Each can infect a new host and grow into another mature, sexually self-sufficient tapeworm.

Humans lack the independence of the timber rattler and the sleek efficiency of the tapeworm. We mature for a decade or more before we can reproduce. We need a complicated series of hormonal changes to start and maintain our reproductive capacity. We exchange genetic material (usually) after an elaborate ritual of courtship and bonding. The nine months of infant development inside the female are demanding and hazardous for mother and offspring alike. Childbirth is no easy matter either, and the extended time devoted to child rearing is greater for humans than for any other species. Still, if such obvious rivals as insects are discounted, humans are among the world's most successful reproducers.

Why Is Reproduction Important?

It isn't, for an individual. An organism may live long and prosper without ever producing more of its own kind. In fact, reproduction may threaten an individual's survival. Consider, for example, trout, which are highly vulnerable to predators when they swim upstream to spawn.

From a species point of view, however, reproduction is imperative. Genetic information must pass from existing organisms to new ones, or that kind of life ends. You, your neighbor, or your best friend may live to a comfortable old age without ever having children. But if everyone did, humankind would become extinct when its last member died.

What Are the Parts of the Human Male Reproductive System?

The most obvious organ of the male reproductive system is the penis, but it is important for reproduction only as a delivery system. What must be delivered are sperm, the male reproductive cells.

When a human male is sexually aroused, the spongy tissues in the penis fill with blood. The organ rises and stiffens, making possible its insertion into the vagina of the female. At climax, or orgasm, muscles contract and propel semen (sperm plus fluid) out

THE HUMAN MALE
REPRODUCTIVE SYSTEM

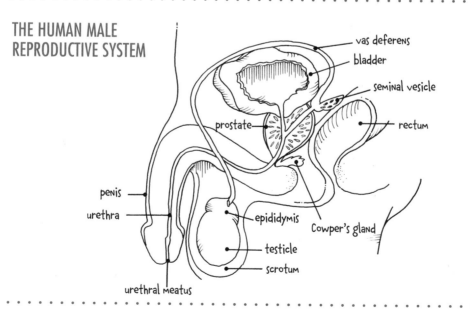

vas deferens
bladder
seminal vesicle
prostate
rectum
penis
urethra
epididymis
Cowper's gland
testicle
scrotum
urethral meatus

of the penis through the urethra, the same tube used for urination. The semen leaves the penis through its external opening, the urethral meatus. This action, ejaculation, drives sperm into the female reproductive system.

The real work of reproduction in the male—the manufacture of sperm—is done silently and invisibly in the testicles. The testicles lie in the scrotum, just behind the penis. They are egg-shaped glands, about 2 inches (5 cm) long and 1 inch (2.5 cm) in diameter.[2]

Covering the testicles are two layers of tissue. One of them extends inward. It forms membrane walls that divide each testicle into about 250 segments, or lobules.[3] Each lobule contains as many as three seminiferous tubules. Each tubule is a tightly coiled tube about 28 inches (70 cm) long. Together, the two testicles contain about 250 yards (230 m) of these tubules.[4]

Above these tubes lie still more coiled tubes, the epididymis, where immature sperm cells develop. The epididymis connects to the vas deferens. This tube is about 18 inches (45 cm) long.[5] It starts at the epididymis and rises into the lower abdomen. It loops over the urinary bladder before receiving fluids from the seminal vesicles, prostate gland, and Cowper's gland. The vas deferens carries the semen to the urethra, where it is expelled during ejaculation.

How Do Sperm Form? The cell divisions that form sperm occur in the seminiferous tubules. Thin walls contain two types of cells. One kind are the spermatogonia. They are immature reproductive cells in varying stages of cell division. The other cell type supports and nourishes the spermatogonia. Spermatogonia develop partially before birth, but lie dormant until puberty. Then, around ages 10–14, as levels of male hormones rise, they begin to divide into sperm cells.

After sperm form in the seminiferous tubules, they move into the epididymis. They grow and mature there for about ten days, then pass into the vas deferens, where they remain until ejaculated. If there is no ejaculation, sperm cells gradually break down and their materials are absorbed and recycled.

Each spermatogonium can produce about 500 sperm over a period of ten weeks.[6] At that rate, you might think the testicles would run out of spermatogonia, but they never do. At least one cell derived from the original spermatogonium "despecializes." It reverts to the undifferentiated form and replaces the parent cell. Then it's ready to make another 500 sperm in a future ten-week period.

What Do Human Sperm Look Like?

On the average, sperm cells measure about 2.5 micrometers across at the head and some 10–20 micrometers long from head to tail.[7] (A micrometer is one-millionth of a meter. For comparison, a human hair measures about 100 micrometers in diameter.)

The sperm's nucleus lies in its head. The front tip is the acrosome. The acrosome contains enzymes that dissolve the egg's protective outer covering during fertilization. (Fertilization, or conception, is the penetration of the female's egg cell by a sperm cell from the male, followed by union of their cell nuclei. The result is a fertilized egg, also called a zygote.) In the midpiece, or "body," of the sperm cell lie the mitochondria. These are the cell's energy conversion factories. They break down the sugar glucose in semen and use its energy to fuel the life and motion of the sperm.

Healthy sperm are energetic swimmers, propelled by their spinning tails. The tail is a bundle of fibers that forms a long, strong filament. A tightly coiled sheath made of spiraled thread surrounds and protects the filament. The rotation of the filament propels the sperm. The sheath helps sperm survive the force of ejaculation, which can reach speeds up to 17 feet (5 m) per second.[8]

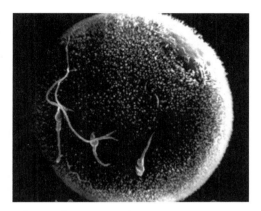

Sperm cluster around an egg moments before fertilization. Only one of them will penetrate the egg's outer membrane.

How Many Sperm Does a Man Ejaculate at One Time?

The average ejaculation is between 2.5 and 5 milliliters of semen. That's a teaspoon or less. Each milliliter contains from 50 to 150 million sperm cells.[9]

If Only One Sperm Fertilizes the Egg, Why Are Millions Ejaculated?

Millions start the journey from the vagina to the egg, but only a few finish it. Most don't survive, and the few that do actually "assist" the single "winner." Penetration of the protective layer that surrounds the egg depends on the chemical action of enzymes from the acrosome. It takes many sperm cells to produce enough of these enzymes to dissolve the barrier.

Are All Sperm Cells Alike? If you are planning a career in science, here's your chance to make a name for yourself. One controversial hypothesis, offered by British biologists Robin Baker and Mark Bellis, says sperm are constructed differently and do different things.[10] According to them, some sperm are "egg-getters." They have the right genetic makeup to fertilize an egg. Others have two heads, two tails, or swim in circles. They form plugs that prevent leakage and prevent sperm from other males from entering the female's reproductive system. While plugs of misshapen, enmeshed sperm cells have been found in the vaginas of females, the rest of the theory remains speculative. A lot of research is needed to refute or confirm it.

What Hormones Regulate Reproduction in Human Males? Male sex hormones are called androgens. Androgens exert several different effects on the male body, including:

- development of male sex organs before birth
- formation of sperm beginning at puberty and continuing throughout adult life
- interest in sexual activity and ability to achieve a sexual response
- stimulation of protein synthesis, leading to the denser bones and greater muscle mass of males as compared with females
- male body shape (wider shoulders and narrower hips than females)
- increased secretions from the skin's oil glands (which can lead to acne during adolescence).

Specific androgens perform specific tasks. Between the ages of 10 and 14 in most males, signs of sexual maturity begin to appear. At that time, the hypothalamus in the brain secretes GnRH (gonadotropin-releasing hormone). GnRH travels to the pituitary gland. There it stimulates the release of the gonadotropins FSH (follicle-stimulating hormone) and LH (luteinizing hormone).

These same hormones are made in females, but they have a different effect in males. LH stimulates cells in the spaces between tubules in the testicles to secrete the hormone testosterone. Testosterone is the main androgen. It causes the voice to deepen and hair to grow on the face, chest, and genitals. Testosterone and FSH cause the testicles to start making sperm cells.

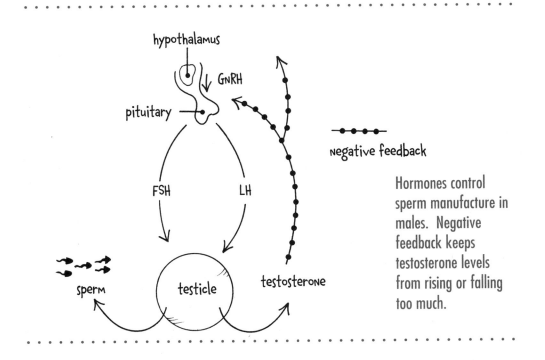

Hormones control sperm manufacture in males. Negative feedback keeps testosterone levels from rising or falling too much.

Cells between the tubules secrete yet another hormone, inhibin. Inhibin sends a message back to the pituitary telling it to make less FSH. Testosterone sends similar messages to the brain, reducing GnRH and LH production. This system of control, called negative feedback, keeps hormone levels balanced. Without them, too much testosterone might be produced.

What Are the Parts of the Human Female Reproductive System?

The organs of female reproduction lie inside the body. The vagina is the hollow tube that opens to the outside, just behind the urethra (where urine leaves the body). During sexual intercourse, the vagina accepts the male penis and the sperm it releases. The vagina is also the tube through which menstrual blood leaves the body when the female is not pregnant. When a child is born, it acts as the birth canal.

Above the vagina lies the hollow, pear-shaped uterus, or womb. It lies between the urinary bladder and the rectum. Before a first pregnancy, it's about as long as an adult's index finger. It weighs about 2 ounces (50 g). During pregnancy, its weight increases to 2.1 pounds (almost a kilogram). Its muscular fibers lengthen more than 100 times, supporting the weight of the growing fetus.[11] The uterus is well supplied with blood. During pregnancy, the blood supply increases so much that the veins that carry blood away from the uterus nearly double their capacity.

Strong ligaments hold the uterus in position. The base of the uterus, the cervix, which normally remains open, shuts tight during pregnancy. It does not open again until the time of birth. The inner lining of the uterus is the endometrium. It undergoes a series of changes

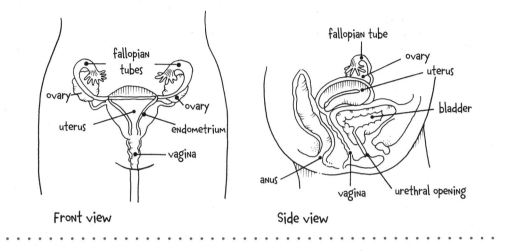

each month in preparation for pregnancy. If no pregnancy occurs, the blood and tissue it builds up are shed as menstrual flow. If pregnancy does occur, the placenta implants into the endometrium. The placenta is the organ that passes food and oxygen to the fetus.

Extending from each side of the uterus are the fallopian tubes. Each is about 4 inches (10 cm) long and about half an inch (1 cm) across.[12] The open, funnel-shaped end of the fallopian tube ends in fingerlike projections. They capture an egg when it is released from an ovary. The egg travels through the tube on its way to the uterus. If sperm are present, the egg will likely be fertilized somewhere in a fallopian tube.

The ovaries are pale-colored, almond-shaped, and about the size of a nine-volt battery. They produce sex hormones and release eggs.

The female ovary contains many follicles, or clusters of cells that surround a developing egg. Follicles and immature eggs are present at birth—about 7 million of them. They lie dormant until puberty. By that time, some 300,000 remain.[13] Then hormonal changes stimulate follicles to become active.

When a girl's menstrual cycle begins, about 20 follicles begin developing each month. Usually, only one of them completes the process, and a single egg is released. (That's about 400 eggs in a woman's reproductive lifetime.[14]) When the egg is mature, hormonal changes cause the follicle to burst open and release the egg. This is ovulation. After ovulation, the ruptured follicle forms a new structure, the corpus luteum. It makes and releases the main female hormone, estrogen. Estrogen causes the inner lining of the uterus to thicken in preparation for a possible pregnancy.

What Hormones Regulate Female Reproduction?

The main female hormone is estrogen. It causes the female sex characteristics that develop at puberty. These include fat deposits in the breasts, belly, hips, and pubic mound; high-pitched voice; broad pelvis; and smooth skin texture lacking facial hair.

Some of the same hormones that work in the male regulate female reproduction, but their effect is different. The hypothalamus in the brain releases gonadotropin-releasing hormone (GnRH). In turn, GnRH stimulates the pituitary gland to secrete follicle-stimulating hormone (FSH) and luteinizing hormone (LH). In the early days of the menstrual cycle, FSH stimulates a follicle to grow and secrete estrogen. Estrogen causes the lining of the uterus to grow and thicken. As the egg

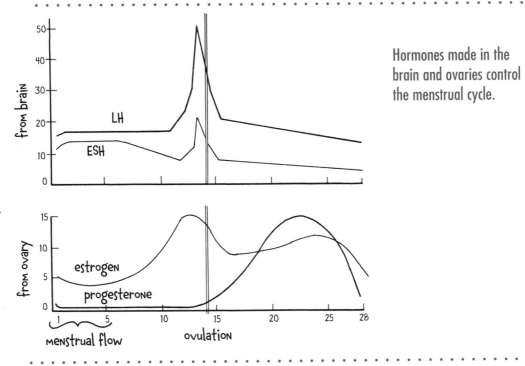

Levels in blood (in arbitrary units)

from brain

from ovary

50
40
30
20
10
0

LH

ESH

15
10
5
0

estrogen

progesterone

1   5   10   15   20   25   28

menstrual flow   ovulation

Hormones made in the brain and ovaries control the menstrual cycle.

nears maturity (around midcycle), high estrogen concentrations cause a surge in LH. The rise in LH stimulates the ovary to release an egg.

After ovulation, decreasing amounts of LH stimulate the corpus luteum to secrete estrogen and another major female hormone, progesterone. Progesterone prepares the uterine lining for implantation of the fertilized egg. If that happens, progesterone maintains the lining throughout the pregnancy and readies the breasts for milk production after birth.

If pregnancy does not occur, the amounts of estrogen and progesterone decrease, and the lining of the uterus is shed as menstrual flow. Between 60 and 250 milliliters of blood, tissue, fluid, mucus, and lining cells are expelled. (That's between two tablespoons and one cup.[15])

Their size and appearance are different, but the most important difference lies in the genetic material, DNA.

In the nuclei of the cells that form sperm and egg, certain proteins, along with the genetic material, DNA, form a loose tangle of material called chromatin. Before cell division begins, chromatin condenses into the rod-shaped bodies, the chromosomes. Each chromosome contains a single DNA molecule. A gene is a segment of that DNA molecule. Humans have about 30,000 genes, distributed among (usually) 46 chromosomes.

Through a series of steps called meiosis, the chromosomes line up in pairs, copy themselves, and then distribute equally among the nuclei of four new cells. (Do the math: 46 chromosomes times 2 divided by 4 = 23). Thus, each new reproductive cell ends up with half the genetic material the parent cell had. Why half? Because sperm and egg fuse to form a new individual. When they do, the complete number of chromosomes is restored (23 +23 = 46).

The 28-day pattern of the menstrual cycle is "predicted" as the "average," but don't expect it to apply to everyone. Normal cycles range from 23 to 35 days.[16] While a contraceptive pill (estrogen mixed with progesterone) makes the cycle predictable and regular, many girls and women not taking the pill have longer or shorter cycles. And the length of their cycle can vary from month to month. Such variation is most likely in the first years of menstruation and before a first pregnancy.

Women vary not only in the length of their cycle, but also in the time when they can become pregnant. Most textbooks say that the fertile period occurs between days 10 and 17 of the menstrual cycle. Researchers at the National Institutes of Health found, however, that more than 70 percent of women have a viable egg in their reproductive system before day 10 or after day 17. "There are few days of the menstrual cycle during which some women are not potentially fertile," they say.[17]

How Does Fertilization Occur?

With a tiny gas explosion, it seems. Stanford University researchers found in sperm cells an enzyme called nitric acid oxidase. It remains inactive inside the head of the sperm cell until a few seconds before fertilization. As the sperm nears the egg, the enzyme starts to work and rapidly produces nitric oxide (NO) gas. The gas is injected into the egg once the cells touch. After about 30 seconds, the influx of NO gas triggers the release of calcium inside the egg. The calcium, in turn, triggers the egg's own nitric acid oxidase to make more NO gas, which releases still more calcium throughout the egg. The rising calcium level stimulates the fertilized egg to begin dividing.[18]

Does the Female System Do Anything to Help Fertilization Happen?

Yes. First, it makes the journey of sperm cells easier—but only when the time is right. During most of the female's menstrual cycle, the mucus made by the cervix is thick and dense. Around the time of ovulation, however, rising estrogen levels cause the mucus to become thin and stretchy (something like egg whites). The mucus then forms channels for the sperm to swim along. Second, the female system feeds the sperm, bathing them in a solution of the sugar glucose, which they use as an energy source. Third, the egg releases chemicals that attract a mere 200 sperm to its surface. Once a sperm binds to the protein coat of an egg, substances called G proteins activate. They trigger the release of enzymes in the egg that allow one sperm to penetrate.[19] Finally, after fertilization, the egg's outer membrane changes chemically, preventing penetration by another sperm cell.

Do Mother and Father Contribute Equally to Their Child's Inheritance?

No, despite the fact that the zygote receives equal numbers of chromosomes from each parent. There are at least four reasons for the inequity:

1. *Sex determination.* Sex is determined by one pair of chromosomes, the so-called sex chromosomes. In humans (but not in all other animals), females usually have two X chromosomes, while males have an X and a Y. When sperm and egg cells form, half get one of the pair of sex chromosomes and half get the other. That means that all egg cells contain an X chromosome, but sperm are different. Half contain an X, and half contain a Y. An egg fertilized by an X-bearing sperm will develop as a female. An egg fertilized by a Y-bearing sperm will develop as a male. Thus, the father determines the sex of the child.

2. *Sex-linked inheritance.* While the Y chromosome contains the genes that determine maleness and some other nonsexual characteristics, it contains fewer genes than the X chromosome. Thus, the male gets more genes from his mother than from his father. Some of them are single genes, lacking a matching partner on the Y. This means certain characteristics are determined by one gene, not two. Such characteristics are called sex-linked, and they are seen most often in males only.

3. *Imprinting.* A fertilized egg contains pairs of genes—one from each parent—but in some pairs, one or the other is inactivated. The mother's or father's gene is there, but it is "turned off." It doesn't work. This process of inactivating some genes and activating others is critical to development. Fertilized eggs do not develop without it. How many imprinted genes are at work in humans—and what they do—are much researched and debated.

4. *Cytoplasmic (or extrachromosomal) inheritance.* Not all DNA is contained in the nucleus. Some lies in structures in the cytoplasm (the material outside the nucleus), especially the mitochondria. There, the chemical reactions that release energy from food occur. In the mitochondria lie small circular DNA molecules. They contain genes that direct the production of proteins important to energy release. In humans, it's the egg, not the sperm, that provides the mitochondria of the zygote. Thus, the zygote gets its energy processing machinery from its mother only.

Are Boys and Girls Born in Equal Numbers?

Among all mammals, including humans, male births slightly outnumber female births. But more females survive, so in the early months or years of life, the ratio evens out. However, among humans, some unexplained discrepancies arise. In Europe, the ratio of male to female births is higher in the south than in the north. In North America, the trend reverses. The ratio is lower in the south than in the north.[20] Possible explanations include smoking (more common in some countries than others), diet, effects of light, virus infections, day length, climate, or mother's age (because older women have more girls). Some experts say the difference is nothing more than a statistical fluke.

How Do Twins, Triplets, and other Multiple Births Happen?

In one of two ways. Fraternal twins (or triplets, quadruplets, or more) develop when two or more eggs are fertilized by two or more sperm. This can happen when the ovaries release more than a single mature egg. These are essentially separate pregnancies, although they develop side-by-side in the mother's uterus. Twins formed this way are no more closely related than any other brothers and sisters. They just happen to share the same birthday. (A more complicated case is when the egg copies itself and divides before fertilization. Then two identical eggs are fertilized by two different sperm.)

Identical twins, triplets, or other multiples form from a single fertilized egg. Sometime during the zygote's early cell divisions, the ball of cells splits once, twice, or more. The separated balls of cells continue to develop normally. Identicals are those twins that are hard to tell apart. They look so much alike because they are genetically identical. Identicals are always the same sex. Fraternals may be the same or different sexes.

What's a Vanishing Twin?

At least 1 in every 20 of us started life sharing the womb with a twin.[21] But, early in pregnancy, the twin embryo "vanished." Its development stopped, and the material in it was absorbed. No one knows what causes a twin to vanish, but it may increase the chance of survival for the remaining embryo. Twins face greater risks of low birth weight and death in the first year of life than single babies do.

Naturally occurring twin births run around 4 in 1,000 births. Expect triplets in 1 of every 7,000 to 10,000. Quadruplets occur once in every 600,000.[22]

The natural rates are coming to mean less and less as more couples are having children later in life and using medical technology to achieve pregnancy. Both of those factors increase the likelihood of a multiple birth. In 2002, 31 in every 1,000 babies in the United States were twins. Eighteen in every 10,000 babies born were triplets or more.[23]

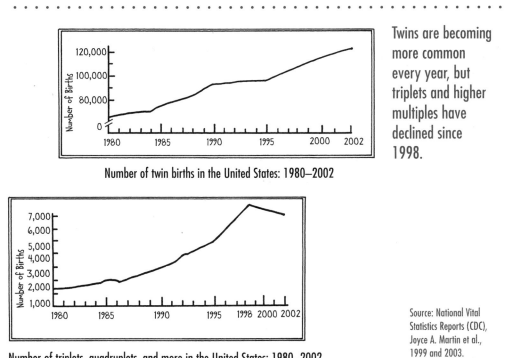

Number of twin births in the United States: 1980–2002

Twins are becoming more common every year, but triplets and higher multiples have declined since 1998.

Number of triplets, quadruplets, and more in the United States: 1980–2002

Source: National Vital Statistics Reports (CDC), Joyce A. Martin et al., 1999 and 2003.

Sex, Stumpies, and Freshwater Snails

·····

Birds do it, bees do it, people do it—in fact, the vast majority of organisms do it—but sexual reproduction often seems more trouble than it's worth.

PAMELA HINES AND ELIZABETH CULOTTA

·····

If you think women have a tough time with pregnancy, pity even more the stumpy-tailed lizard of Australia. There's nothing remarkable about the lizard's life. It's common over most of Australia, eats almost everything, and grows to about 16 inches (40 cm) long. Unlike lizards that lay eggs, young stumpies develop much as mammals do—inside the female's body, attached by a placenta. But this "pregnancy" brings untold hazards to the mother stumpy. During the last month, she seldom eats, scarcely breathes, and hardly moves.[24]

The reason is size, says University of Adelaide researcher Suzy Munns. Carrying from one to four babies, the female stumpy doesn't get any bigger during her five to six months' term. The young simply take up more and more space inside the mother's body cavity, squashing her lungs and digestive system. "Baby stumpies can grow as large as 35 percent of the mother's body weight," says Munns. "If a human female were to give birth to a baby that [large], it would mean giving birth to a child the size of an average six-year-old!"[25]

Why should the stumpy go to all this trouble? In fact, why should any animal bother to reproduce sexually at all? Asexual reproduction—requiring only one parent—seems far simpler and more efficient. Bacteria, yeast, and fungi are perfect asexual reproducers. Bacteria split in two,

Researcher Suzy Munns with stumpies

doubling their numbers in minutes. Yeast bud, and fungi form spores. They can produce thousands of exact duplicates of themselves in hours, with little pain or effort required.

Sexual reproduction, by comparison, is a new invention. It is difficult, slow, and prone to error. Sperm and egg cells must be produced, each containing precisely half the genetic material in the nucleus of each parent cell. Opportunities for mutations (errors in copying DNA) crop up when reproductive cells form. Getting sperm and egg together introduces the complications of finding a mate and exchanging genetic material. All that trouble produces fewer offspring than asexual reproduction.

Nonetheless, asexual reproduction is rare, but sexual reproduction is common. "Look out the window," says University of California at Santa Barbara scientist William Rice, "and almost every organism you see reproduces sexually."[26] The stumpy-tailed lizard might well ask why, as have many biologists.

Indiana University researcher Curt Lively approached the question with studies of a freshwater snail that lives in the glacial lakes of New Zealand's South Island. The snail is a perfect animal for this research because it reproduces both sexually and asexually. Asexual snails make large numbers of exact copies of themselves. The sexual ones, like all other sexually reproducing organisms, produce smaller numbers of offspring that show mixes of their parents' characteristics.

Lively found that, in lakes with few parasites that preyed on the snails, asexual populations flourished; but where parasites were abundant, the sexual snails thrived. Lively thinks that the constantly changing mix of genes among the sexual snails gives them a survival advantage. By chance, some inherit a combination of genetic traits that allows them to resist the attack of parasites. These survivors become the parents of the next generation, passing along their adaptive advantage to their offspring. That wouldn't be possible in an asexually reproducing population where all are genetically the same and equally vulnerable to parasites.[27]

A slightly different theory of sex developed in the work of William Rice and Adam Chippindale at the University of California, Santa

Barbara. Using genetic engineering, they created different populations of fruit flies. Some of them mixed genes sexually, and some did not. They tracked a mutation of a gene that coded for red eyes instead of white eyes in the flies. White-eyed males were blind, so at a disadvantage. They were less able to find mates under the laboratory's lighted conditions.

In the sexually reproducing flies, the red eye gene showed up with increasing frequency over the generations, eventually reaching all the flies. The number of red-eyed flies grew in the asexual populations too, but not as rapidly. The spread of the gene usually stopped before showing up in all the flies.[28] The sexual population "gets the good gene faster," Rice says.[29]

It seems that sex does two things: It accumulates good mutations and eliminates bad ones. "My view is they're both going on," says Graham Bell of McGill University in Montreal. "Something as complex, onerous, and laborious as sexuality is probably only going to be maintained if it's doing something very important."[30]

No doubt, stumpy-tailed lizards would agree.

CHAPTER TWO

26 QUESTIONS

ABOUT PREGNANCY
AND CHILDBIRTH

*If newborns could remember and speak, they would emerge
from the womb carrying tales as wondrous as Homer's.*
• SHARON BEGLEY •
(in *Newsweek*)

How Do Pregnancy Tests Work?

Within the first week after a zygote implants in the wall of the uterus, the developing placenta begins to produce the hormone hCG (human chorionic gonadotropin). This hormone enters the woman's bloodstream and travels to the ovaries. There it triggers the release of the estrogen and progesterone needed to maintain the pregnancy. Some hCG is excreted in the urine.

Laboratory and at-home pregnancy tests use antibodies to detect hCG, either in the blood or in the urine. Antibodies are proteins made by the immune system in response to a foreign protein. The antibodies

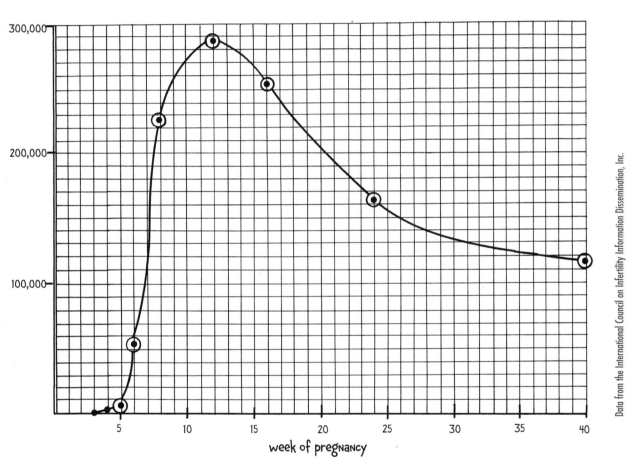

300,000

200,000

100,000

5   10   15   20   25   30   35   40

week of pregnancy

Data from the International Council on Infertility Information Dissemination, Inc.

Human chorionic gonadotropin (hCG) levels during pregnancy

in pregnancy tests are manufactured in the blood of mice. They are isolated from the mouse blood and put onto a test strip, along with an enzyme that causes a color change when antibodies and hCG molecules combine. The color change shows that hCG is present. That's a positive test for pregnancy.

The level of hCG in the blood starts small, but doubles every two or three days in early pregnancy, reaching its peak between the eighth and twelfth weeks.[1] Tests done too soon after a missed period may fail to detect 10 percent or more of pregnancies.[2] More than 100 different do-it-yourself pregnancy test kits are available without a prescription. In 1999, Americans bought 19 million of them.[3]

How Long Does Pregnancy Last?

The average pregnancy lasts 280 days, or 40 weeks from the first day of the last menstrual period. Since about 14 days pass before an egg is fertilized, the development from zygote to birth actually requires 266 days. Thus, a woman is officially two weeks pregnant when egg and sperm fuse, and the fourth week of pregnancy is actually the second week of embryonic development.

Why Don't Pregnant Women Have Periods?

The embryo implants in the lining of the uterus. Through the placenta attached to it, the fetus is nourished and provided with oxygen. The implantation changes hormone levels. High levels of progesterone secreted by the corpus luteum tell the brain to decrease its production of GnRH, FSH, and LH. This balance of hormones maintains the uterine lining and prevents it from shedding. (Conversely, when pregnancy ends or does not occur, low levels of progesterone stimulate the secretion of GnRH, FSH, and LH and bring on the menstrual flow.)

How Much and How Fast Does a Zygote Grow?

The fertilized egg, or zygote, is smaller than the period at the end of this sentence. During pregnancy, the zygote increases its cell numbers to more than 200 million. Weight increases by a factor of 6 billion![4]

Although the fetus gains the most weight in the last two months of pregnancy, the rate of growth is actually greater in the early weeks. During the first month of pregnancy, fetal weight increases 10,000 times. In the second month, the increase is 74 times. By the third month, the multiplier has dropped to 11.[5]

What Happens in the Early Weeks of Pregnancy?

The first 14 weeks of pregnancy are called the first trimester.

About 30 hours after egg and sperm unite (about 15 days of pregnancy), the fertilized egg, or zygote, begins to divide. One cell becomes two, then four, and then eight. These early divisions happen while the zygote is traveling through the fallopian tube toward the uterus. Some of the cells of the zygote divide more rapidly than others, so that by the third day of development, the zygote contains 12 cells of unequal size. This stage is called the morula.

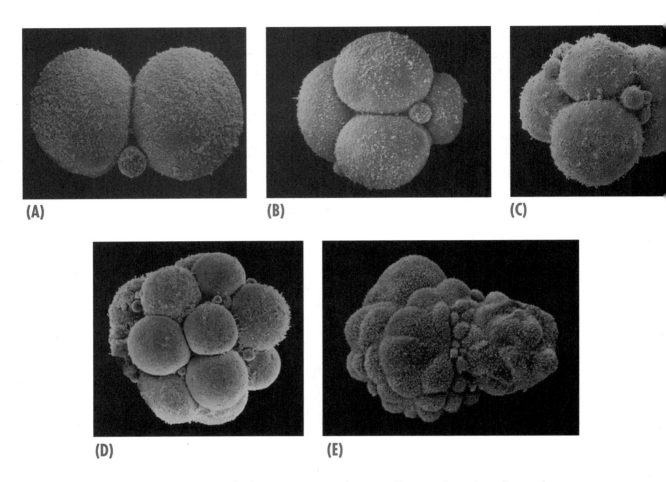

(A) A microscopic image of a human zygote at the two-cell stage, about thirty hours after fertilization. (The smaller spherical structure between the cells at the bottom is called a polar body. It will eventually degrade.) **(B)** About forty hours after fertilization, the zygote has undergone two cell divisions and is now four cells. **(C)** Another division produces eight cells. **(D)** Three days after fertilization, the zygote is a morula with 12 cells. **(E)** Five days after fertilization, it is a blastocyst—a hollow ball of cells with a fluid center. Most of these cells will form the placenta and membranes, and only a small group (the inner mass) will form the embryo itself. The blastocyst is now ready to implant in the uterus.

As unequal cell division continues, a cavity forms inside the morula. There are no cells there, only fluid. Now, the zygote is called a blastocyst. This is an important stage, because the cells are beginning to specialize. Those lying inside the blastocyst will become the embryo itself. Those on the outside will form the placenta. (The placenta is the organ that will later implant and grow inside the uterus. It will handle the exchange of food, oxygen, and waste materials between the mother and the embryo.)

About six days after fertilization, implantation begins. The process is something like "a tennis ball rolling over a tabletop covered with syrup," says University of California San Francisco scientist Susan Fisher.[6] The blastocyst is coated with a protein called L-secretin. Carbohydrate molecules (similar to sugars and starches) line the uterus. As the blastocyst rolls along, the L-secretin molecules latch onto the carbohydrates. This slows the "rolling ball" to a stop.

After implantation, cells of the blastocyst's outer layer invade the lining of the uterus. There, invasion erodes its walls of tiny capillaries, allowing oxygen and food from the mother's blood to diffuse into the embryo. The invasion, along with the hormone progesterone from the corpus luteum in the ovary, causes the uterine lining to build up a supply of fats and complex sugars. These materials serve as an energy source for the developing blastocyst.

On the 14th day after fertilization (week four of the pregnancy, but the woman has not yet missed a menstrual period), the blastocyst gets a name change. It is now an embryo. Because of its flat, round shape, it is called the embryonic disc. It lies between two other structures, the amniotic cavity and the yolk sac. Cells have moved from the outside inward, forming two layers. In the weeks to come, the inner layer, or endoderm, will become the embryo's digestive, respiratory, and excretory systems. The outermost cells, the ectoderm, will become the skin and nervous system.

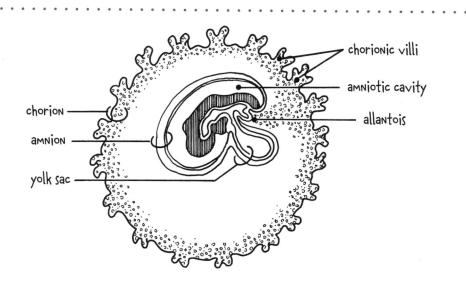

chorionic villi

amniotic cavity

allantois

chorion

amnion

yolk sac

The embryo at four weeks. Notice the membranes and the chorionic villi.

Four membranes now surround the embryo. They are the yolk sac, allantois, amnion, and chorion. Despite its name, the yolk sac contains no yolk, only fluid. It may play a role in getting nutrients to the embryonic disc. The allantois grows out from the yolk sac. It is one of several sites of early blood formation. It eventually disappears inside the embryo, forming part of the umbilical cord. The amnion initially surrounds the embryo. It later becomes filled with clear fluid. The fluid provides cushioning, allows for movement, helps the lungs develop, stabilizes temperature, and provides a barrier against infection. The chorion surrounds the amnion and eventually fuses with it. It becomes the embryo portion of the placenta. Its fingerlike projections form the primary chorionic villi of the placenta. As the embryo's circulatory system grows, blood vessels will crowd the spaces inside the villi. Their large surface area allows for maximum movement of oxygen, food, and waste materials.

The prechordal plate forms in week four of the pregnancy. It is where the head end of the embryo will develop. Along the embryonic disc, a line forms. It is called the primitive streak. It starts at the embryo's tail end and moves toward the prechordal plate at the head. Further movement and specialization of cells along the prechordal plate form the notochord. It is a stiff ridge of cells where the backbone will later develop.

In the fifth week of pregnancy, the embryo's shape changes. It stretches into a longer, slimmer form. This is when gastrulation occurs. Gastrulation is the movement of another layer of cells into the interior. This infolding creates the middle cell layer, the mesoderm. The mesoderm on both sides of the notochord thickens, forming somites. In later stages of development, the somites will become the bones and muscles of arms and legs. The formation of blood vessels also begins at this time, and the embryo's primitive heart starts beating. It contains only two chambers and is no bigger than a poppy seed.

Toward the end of the fifth week, neurulation

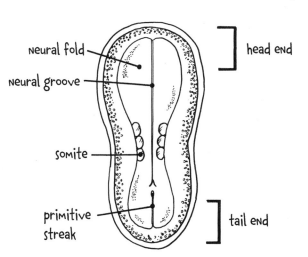

The embryo in the fifth week. The somites will become arms and legs. The neural groove will develop into the spinal cord.

begins. The notochord grows longer, and two folds of ectoderm rise like mountain ridges along the embryo's back. Between these ridges, the neural folds, lies a depression, the neural groove. The edges of the folds grow together across the groove and fuse, forming the neural tube.

By the end of the sixth week, neurulation is complete. Neural tube cells have begun to develop as brain and spinal cord. Also in that week, the buds that will become arms and legs appear. The upper and lower jaw begin to develop, as do eyes, inner ears, and windpipe.

In the seventh week, the placenta and umbilical cord are fully functional. The umbilical cord connects the embryo to the placenta. It contains two arteries that carry oxygen and nutrients to the embryo and one large vein that carries waste products away. The embryo's head grows faster than other body regions, because the brain and facial structures are organizing rapidly. The upper limb buds are paddle-shaped. The lower limb buds look like flippers. Pigment appears where the eyes will be. Pits form where the nostrils will be. The shape of thigh, calf, and foot begin to appear in the leg limb buds.

In the eighth week, fingers begin forming, but it's another week before toes appear. The embryo moves, twitching its body and limb buds. The shell-shaped external ear structure begins to appear. The neck begins to form.

In the ninth week, eyelids and the outer ears become visible. The heart divides into four chambers. Digestive, excretory, and reproductive organs have begun to form. Development of arms and legs is rapid. So is the growth of the intestines.

At ten weeks, the embryo measures 1 inch (2.5 cm) long. It changes its name again. From now until birth, it's called a fetus. By the tenth week, testes or ovaries have developed internally, although sex is not apparent on the outside. Bones begin to harden in the leg. Eyelids become visible, but are fused shut.

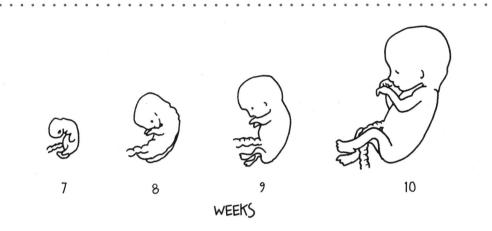

WEEKS

Growth in the early weeks is rapid.

Between weeks 11 and 14, growth of the body, in relation to the head, speeds up. The fetal form lengthens into a more balanced-looking shape. Bones begin to form in the skull. Sex organs develop externally, and it's possible to tell male from female. Blood cells are manufactured. Urine is made and excreted into the amniotic fluid. In this time, the fetus grows to a length of about 4 inches (10 cm). Its weight? A little more than an ounce (30 g).

What Happens in the Later Months of Pregnancy?

The second trimester of pregnancy is 14 to 28 weeks, or the fourth through sixth months. In month four, the volume of amniotic fluid increases greatly. So do the fetal requirements for food, water, and oxygen—all delivered through the umbilical cord. Hair grows on the skull and eyebrows.

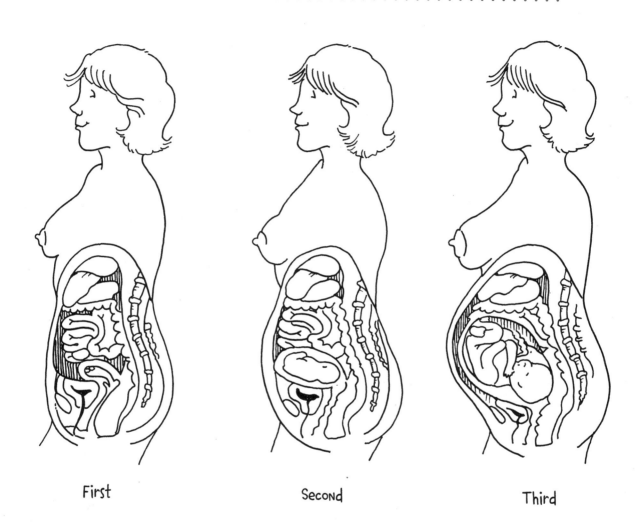

First

Second

Third

The trimesters of pregnancy

The skin is furred with silky fine hair, called lanugo. The heartbeat is stronger and twice as fast as the mother's. The fetus sleeps, wakes, swallows, and urinates. Some fetuses even suck their thumbs.

In the fifth month, many women report the first sensation of fetal movement, which may feel like a flutter, tickle, or bubbles. The fetus is now about 6½ inches (nearly 17 cm) long. It weighs about 12 ounces (almost 350 g). It can hear and make breathing movements, although no air can be drawn into the lungs until after birth. The facial features are wrinkled and shriveled looking.

In the sixth month, movement is stronger and more persistent. The pregnant woman now describes sensations of kicking, punching, or turning. The six-month fetus coughs, hiccups, and startles in response to loud noises.

The third trimester is from 28 to 40 weeks, or months seven through nine. Month seven is a period of rapid fetal growth. The fetus grows to a weight of about 3 pounds (1.5 kg) or more. It makes faces and crying movements, although not the sounds. The eyes open, and taste buds form in the mouth. The fetus may turn head down during the seventh month and stay in that position until birth.

In months eight and nine, the uterus expands to 1,000 times its nonpregnant size.[7] The fetus gains more than half its birth weight. It grows so large that some women can feel the shape of head, feet, and arms through their abdomens. Fingernails and toenails grow so much that they may need trimming at birth. The fetal bones harden in these months, but the joints of the skull will not close completely until after birth. As the end of pregnancy draws near, the fetus grows to its full-term weight of about 7 pounds (around 3 kg).

A substance called meconium forms in the intestines. It will be the first bowel movement after birth.

What Medical Care Should a Woman Get Before Pregnancy?

Any woman who has a chance of getting pregnant needs to make sure she's healthy before pregnancy occurs. That means visiting a doctor, clinic, or health professional for regular physicals. During a first visit, the health care provider typically records a health history. It includes confidential information on sexual activity, past pregnancies, sexually transmitted infections, ongoing medical conditions such as diabetes, use of contraceptives to prevent pregnancy, and use of tobacco, alcohol, and drugs.

A complete physical exam involves checking weight, blood pressure, thyroid, heart, lungs, breasts, and abdomen. Protein, bacteria, blood, or sugar detected in urine may indicate a health problem. A Pap smear, in which a sample of cells is taken from the base of the uterus and examined under a microscope, can reveal changes in the cervix that can lead to cancer. The Pap test also detects viral infections such as HPV (human papilloma virus).

A routine medical exam is a good opportunity to discuss preventing pregnancy and guarding against sexually transmitted diseases. It's also a good time to get help with any threats to health—such as smoking, taking street drugs, or drinking alcohol—and to learn about good nutrition and weight control.

What Medical Care Should a Woman Get During Pregnancy?

Good prenatal care starts with a health history and a physical exam. Health care providers usually see a healthy woman every month early in pregnancy, with visits spaced closer together as the pregnancy advances. Appointments are scheduled more often if the woman had trouble becoming pregnant, is over age 35, is carrying more than one fetus, has a high risk of birth defects, or has a health problem such as diabetes or high blood pressure. At each visit, weight and blood pressure are measured. Urine is checked for protein and glucose. Feet and hands are checked for signs of swelling. Health care providers measure the size of the uterus and check the fetal heartbeat, to make sure growth and development are on schedule.

Many women's health specialists send a pregnant woman to get a sonogram (also called ultrasound) once, twice, or several times during a pregnancy. A sonogram is a series of images captured by a device called an ultrasound scanner. The scanner uses sound waves to create the pictures. Doctors get sonograms to verify the age of the fetus and to check the development of its bones and organs. Sonograms also help health care providers look for uterine problems, birth defects, or multiple fetuses.

Blood samples drawn at different times during the pregnancy are sent to a lab for testing. Their results may reveal problems such as anemia or Rh incompatibility. Rh incompatibility can occur when the woman does not have a blood protein named Rh in her blood (she is Rh-negative), but the fetus does (it is Rh-positive). In such cases, antibodies in the mother's blood may attack and destroy fetal blood cells. A simple treatment prevents the disease. It involves injecting a substance that neutralizes the antibodies. (Read more on page 113.)

In many states, the law requires testing the mother's blood for HIV (the virus that causes AIDS) during pregnancy. If HIV is found, the woman is treated with antiviral drugs to help prevent transmission of the virus to her child. Also, the child is treated against HIV immediately after birth.

Sometime between 15 and 22 weeks, a blood sample from the mother is taken for maternal serum screening (also called multiple marker or quadruple screen). The test measures the levels of four proteins in the blood that may be signs of birth defects in the fetus. An unusual result doesn't diagnose a birth defect, but it may indicate a need for another test, amniocentesis. To perform this test, a small amount of amniotic fluid is withdrawn from the uterus. Floating in it are some fetal cells. They can be grown in the laboratory and then analyzed.

As delivery draws near, a sample of cells from the vagina is checked for the presence of the Group B streptococcus (GBS) bacteria. They can be present in the woman without symptoms, but if they pass to the baby at birth, they can cause serious illness, even death. Antibiotics given before and during labor prevent that.

Should a Pregnant Woman Eat For Two?

Yes, but that doesn't mean double. Pregnant women should eat three light, healthy meals daily, with healthy snacks in between if necessary. Skipping meals or going a long time without food stresses the body and increases the risk of early delivery.

A healthy weight gain is 25 to 35 pounds (about 11 to 16 kg) over the nine months of pregnancy. It doesn't take much extra food to do that. In early pregnancy, an extra 100 to 200 calories a day are all that's needed. (One large apple or a slice of wheat bread provides about 100 calories.) Later in pregnancy, requirements increase to about 300 extra calories a day. That's about the number in a medium baked potato sprinkled with a spoonful of cheese.

While the body's need for food doesn't double, its need for iron does. Calcium is a concern too, particularly since many young women don't get enough even when they're not pregnant. Another important

NUTRIENTS IMPORTANT DURING PREGNANCY

NUTRIENT	NEEDED FOR	GOOD SOURCES
Water	Fetal cell development, maintaining blood volume, and using many nutrients. Helps the pregnant woman avoid bladder infections, constipation, and swelling of the feet and ankles.	Milk, fruit juice, water.
Protein	Building the structure of cells.	Eggs, lean meat, skim milk, yogurt, cheese, peanut butter, dried beans.
Fats	Energy. Also needed for the absorption of several important vitamins, including A and D.	Cheese, peanut butter, egg, avocado, olive oil. Needed in small quantities only.
Carbohydrates	Energy. Fiber prevents constipation in the pregnant woman.	Whole-grain breads and cereals, tortillas, pasta, rice, potato, corn.
Vitamin A	Forming skin, bones, eyes, and internal organs.	Vegetable juice, skim milk, cantaloupe, peaches, spinach.
Vitamin C	Making collagen, blood proteins, bone, cartilage, and muscle.	Citrus fruits, broccoli, cauliflower, tomatoes.
Vitamin D	Building bones, muscle, and teeth and facilitating nerve and muscle action.	Skim milk, eggs, sardines, salmon.
Folic acid (a B vitamin)	Making DNA in fetal cells. An adequate amount reduces the risk of neural tube birth defects and cleft lip and palate.	Kale, broccoli, asparagus, lean beef, lentils, peanuts, bread, pasta.
Calcium	Building bones and teeth.	Skim milk, cheese, yogurt, salad greens, salmon, sardines.
Iron	Making the oxygen-carrying compound in blood, hemoglobin.	Dried fruits, lean meat, dried beans, pasta, whole-grain breads, dark-green vegetables.
Zinc	DNA synthesis and cell growth.	Whole-grain breads and cereals, lean meat, milk, seafood.

nutrient is the B vitamin folic acid. Low levels of folic acid cause serious birth defects, and the damage is done even before the woman realizes she is pregnant. For these reasons, many health care providers recommend a daily multiple vitamin and mineral pill for all women and girls.

By the way, good nutrition is as important for fathers as it is for mothers. Several studies have linked low levels of folic acid and zinc in men to low sperm counts and chromosome breaks in sperm cells.[8] When Dutch researchers gave zinc and folate supplements to men with low sperm counts, they found a 74 percent increase in the number of normal sperm in the men's semen.[9]

Are There Some Foods Pregnant Women Shouldn't Eat?

Because pregnancy reduces immunity slightly, pregnant women need to be especially careful about foodborne infections. The *Listeria* organism, which lives in meats and in unpasteurized milk and juices, offers one good example. Listeria causes nausea, stomach cramps, and fever. During pregnancy, it can have more serious consequences, including miscarriage and stillbirth. Pregnant women should avoid cheeses made from unpasteurized milk such as Brie, Camembert, and Roquefort. They should not eat raw or undercooked eggs and products that may contain raw eggs, such as Caesar salad dressing and unbaked, homemade cookie dough. That's because raw eggs may contain *Salmonella*. The organism won't hurt the fetus, but it makes pregnant women very sick with diarrhea, fever, cramps, headache, nausea, and vomiting. Because fatty fishes such as shark, swordfish, tilefish, and king mackerel contain high levels of mercury, they are best left off the menu until after delivery. Tuna should be limited to 6 ounces (one small can) a week. Mercury can cause birth defects and miscarriage (loss of a pregnancy).

Should Pregnant Women Drink Coffee?

The caffeine in coffee, tea, and colas has been linked to miscarriage, premature labor, low birth weight, and sudden infant death. For those reasons, in 1980, the Food and Drug Administration issued a warning advising pregnant women to avoid caffeine. Since no one is sure about a safe amount, its probably best to stay away from tea, coffee, and soft drinks that contain caffeine. Decaffeinated coffee actually contains some caffeine, so it is best avoided too. The best drink for pregnant women? Water.

Can a Pregnant Woman Get Away With Smoking?

Everyone knows a pregnant woman who has "gotten away with smoking" during pregnancy. Her baby was born with no apparent defect. But did she really "get away with smoking," and can other women assume they'll be equally "lucky"? The answer is "no" on both counts. Researchers at Carolinas Medical Center measured the heart rate of newborns, all apparently healthy. Their appearance was deceiving. Those born to mothers who had smoked during pregnancy showed signs of nicotine withdrawal. Their hearts beat more rapidly than those of their smoke-free peers.[10]

Smoking doubles the risk of low birth weight, a major cause of illness and infant death.[11] Fetal growth is slowed, maybe because the amount of oxygen available to the fetus is lessened. Smokers have more stillbirths. They face a greater risk of SIDS (sudden infant death syndrome, or death of a baby during sleep from an unknown cause). Evidence suggests that the mother's smoking may also do permanent damage to the developing fallopian tubes of her unborn, female child. Effects on the reproductive organs of the male fetus aren't known.

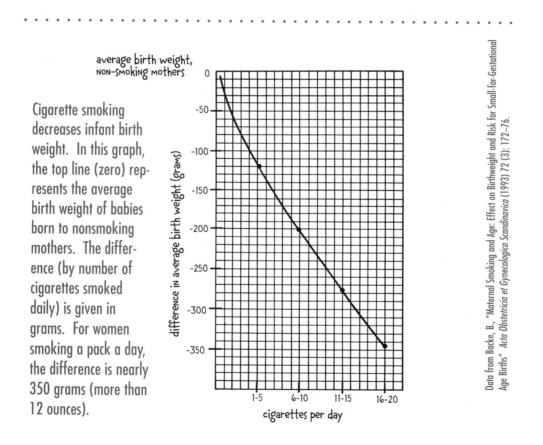

Cigarette smoking decreases infant birth weight. In this graph, the top line (zero) represents the average birth weight of babies born to nonsmoking mothers. The difference (by number of cigarettes smoked daily) is given in grams. For women smoking a pack a day, the difference is nearly 350 grams (more than 12 ounces).

Data from Backe, B., "Maternal Smoking and Age: Effect on Birthweight and Risk for Small-for-Gestational Age Births" Acta Obstetricia et Gynecologica Scandinavica (1993) 72 (3): 172–76.

Alcohol causes the serious birth defect fetal alcohol syndrome. Because it is a small molecule, alcohol quickly enters the mother's blood and crosses through the placenta into the fetus. A liver of a tiny fetus cannot break down alcohol the way its mother's liver can. Alcohol damages microglial cells in the brain. Microglial cells are disease fighters and "trash collectors." It suppresses the growth and maturation of the central nervous system, leading to learning and behavioral problems in infants and children. The symptoms of fetal alcohol syndrome include mental retardation, physical impairments, and (often) hyperactivity and a short attention span. "Fetal alcohol syndrome is a totally preventable birth defect," says Karen Hymbaugh of the National Center on Birth Defects and Developmental Disabilities at the Centers for Disease Control in Atlanta.[12] Avoiding alcohol altogether prevents both the syndrome and its milder form, fetal alcohol effect. Any woman who may become pregnant, even "accidentally," needs to abstain from alcohol. Those who consumed alcohol in the early weeks before they realized they were pregnant need to discuss the situation honestly with their health care providers.

As with alcohol, any woman who has taken any drug in the early weeks of pregnancy needs to discuss the situation honestly with a health care provider. Some drugs are safe, while others may threaten both infant and maternal survival.

Illegal "street" drugs that are addictive affect the fetus directly and indirectly. The direct effects are obvious. Infants are born addicted. The lucky ones go through painful withdrawal. The unlucky ones die. The indirect effects arise from the mother's inability to care for herself. She may eat poorly and neglect prenatal medical care. If she shares needles with other addicts who inject drugs, she may contract HIV, the virus that causes AIDS. HIV may pass through the placenta and infect the fetus.

Even one use of a drug like cocaine during pregnancy can lead to miscarriage, fetal brain damage, and death of fetus or mother. Surviving infants may be born premature and underweight. The effects are long-lasting. Researchers at Case Western University tested children whose mothers used cocaine during pregnancy. The children looked normal, but they developed more slowly and learned with greater difficulty than children whose mothers had not taken cocaine.[13]

Drugs need not be illegal to be dangerous during pregnancy. Aspirin, cold medicines, and acne preparations can injure the fetus. Some "natural" herbal supplements and teas aren't safe either. The herb goldenseal, for example, is said to relieve colds, flu, and stomach upsets. Pregnant women should avoid it, however, because it stimulates contractions of the uterus.

Some drugs are indispensable during pregnancy. Disorders such as high blood pressure, diabetes, epilepsy, AIDS, and asthma pose a greater threat if left untreated than if treated, so doctors usually prescribe medications to control them. For example, the antiviral drug AZT reduces by two thirds the risk that an HIV-positive mother (infected with the virus that causes AIDS) will transmit the virus to her unborn child.

However, even prescription drugs must be handled with caution. It's difficult for doctors to know precisely what the risks of drugs are, especially those that are newly available. "The safety of new agents cannot be known with certainty until a drug has been on the market for many years," says Dr. Karen Lasser, a researcher at Harvard Medical School.[14] Since only one in every hundred drugs has been proven safe during pregnancy, it pays to be suspicious of them all.[15]

SOME DRUGS AND THEIR EFFECTS ON THE EMBRYO OR FETUS

DRUG	EFFECTS ON FETUS
Acetaminophen (pain-reliever)	Normal doses are considered safe, but an overdose can induce malformations caused by excess amniotic fluid.
Aspirin	Bleeding inside the skull.
Alcohol	Small head, slow growth, abnormal facial features, mental impairment.
Amitryptyline (an antidepressant)	Small jaw, limb reduction.
Antithyroid drugs	Goiter.
Caffeine	Defects of bones, muscles, and kidneys.
Codeine (e.g., in cough syrup)	Fluid around the brain; defects of heart, lungs, mouth, bones, and muscles.
Coumadin (an anticlotting drug)	Spina bifida, heart disease, growth retardation, bleeding.
Diazepam (antianxiety drug)	Spina bifida, heart defects, cleft lip and palate.
Haloperidol (antipsychotic)	Limb deformities.
Isotretinoin (the acne medicine Accutane)	Mental retardation, heart abnormalities.
LSD (causes hallucination in users)	Fluid around the brain, limb deficiencies.
Marijuana	Retarded growth, abnormal brain development, nervous system damage.
Methotrexate (treats cancer and arthritis)	Slow growth, abnormalities of jaw and ears, heart defects, death.
Phenobarbitol (epilepsy and insomnia)	Fluid in the skull, slow growth, abnormalities of fingers and toes.
Tobacco	Retarded growth.

Should a Pregnant Woman Exercise??

For most pregnant women, regular exercise is just as beneficial as it is for everyone else. It helps prevent heart disease, high blood pressure, diabetes, depression, osteoporosis ("brittle bone" disease), and maybe even some kinds of cancer. Exercise offers some added benefits during pregnancy, including relief from constipation, backache, fatigue, and varicose veins.

Sensible exercise is important during pregnancy. These women are in a prenatal yoga class.

Healthy women who exercised before pregnancy can continue at a moderate level, says the American College of Obstetricians and Gynecologists.[16] As long as the pregnancy progresses normally, 30 minutes or more a day of such activities as walking, swimming, or cycling on a stationary bicycle are good for both mother and fetus. Many doctors suggest, however, that strenuous exercise—while not dangerous—is best postponed, as it can lead to a modest reduction in fetal weight. Because of the risk of accident or impact injury, water-skiing, diving, snowmobiling, horseback riding, and skiing are best avoided.

Women who have not exercised before pregnancy may want to increase their level of activity, but pregnancy is not the time to start training for the Olympics. Exercise is not a good idea for pregnant women who

- have high blood pressure, diabetes, heart disease, thyroid disease, or other major medical problems.
- have had a miscarriage or early delivery of a previous baby.
- experience bleeding or have ruptured membranes.
- have a weak or "incompetent" cervix. (The cervix is called "incompetent" if it fails to close during pregnancy.)

How Does a Woman's Body Change During Pregnancy?

Most pregnant women experience some of the following changes in their bodies:

- increased salivation
- headache
- fatigue
- heartburn, or a stinging sensation in the upper abdomen, resulting from the rise of stomach acid into the esophagus. (This happens because the enlarging uterus prevents expansion of the stomach after eating.)

- a runny or stuffy nose, resulting from the swelling of membranes in the nose and throat
- inflammation or bleeding of the gums (Estrogen increases the blood supply and thickness of gums.)
- "morning sickness," nausea, loss of appetite, vomiting
- swollen feet and ankles resulting from accumulation of fluids
- varicose veins in the legs, which worsen as the pregnancy progresses and in subsequent pregnancies
- increased susceptibility of the joints to injury, because high hormone levels relax tendons and ligaments, especially toward the end of pregnancy
- enlargement of veins and growth of fat deposits in the breasts
- erection of the nipples and firming of the areolae (areas of darkened skin around the nipples)
- constipation and frequent urination, resulting from pressure of the enlarging uterus on the intestines and bladder
- waddling walk and unsteady balance, because the body's center of gravity changes
- backaches and muscle strain from supporting the extra weight in the abdomen
- darkening of skin of the face, nipples, and vulva (external female genitals) and a dark line extending from the navel downward on the abdomen
- "stretch marks" resulting from rapid growth of the fetus in the abdomen and increased storage of fat under the skin of the abdomen, breasts, thighs, and buttocks
- complexion changes resulting from hormonal shifts, so that acne either improves or worsens
- hair loss or changes in hair texture
- emotional highs and lows, mood shifts.

What Is
Labor?

Labor is the process of giving birth, ending in the emergence of the infant, or delivery. Although no two births are identical, the stages in the process are the same:

Prelabor: The uterus begins to contract painfully and predictably (different from the irregular, painless contractions felt earlier in pregnancy). If it hasn't already, the mucus plug that has blocked the cervix for nine months passes out through the vagina. Now, or later as labor intensifies, the sac of amniotic fluid breaks, releasing a gush or a trickle of clear liquid. The cervix grows shorter, a process called effacement. Before effacement, it's about 1 inch (2 cm) long. After effacement, it's paper-thin.

Gradually, contractions grow stronger, more frequent, and longer-lasting. The cervix begins to open, or dilate. Prelabor can go on for eight hours or more before the opening of the cervix reaches a diameter of 4 centimeters (about 1.5 inches). That's when active labor officially starts, and help from a doctor or midwife usually begins.

Active labor: Contractions become more frequent, averaging two or three minutes apart. They also last longer, perhaps a minute or more. The cervix opens faster during this time, eventually reaching its fully open diameter of 10 centimeters (4 inches). While this is happening, the fetus is descending into the pelvic area. This puts pressure on the rectum, and makes some women feel as if they are going to have a bowel movement. Some women shake, shiver, feel nauseous, or vomit during active labor. At this time, contractions become painful enough that some women request anesthesia (pain relief).

Delivery: Once the cervix is fully open, contractions slow and become more powerful. They push the fetus down into the birth canal. Some health care providers encourage women to contract their abdominal muscles at this time. This "pushing" speeds the descent of the fetus. A brief period of relaxation follows each contraction, and the fetus slips back a little each time. The perineum, the tissue between the vaginal opening and the anus, bulges with each contraction, and the top of the head emerges. "Crowning" happens when the widest part of the head becomes visible. After the entire head delivers, health care providers usually suction fluids from the baby's mouth and nose. The baby's head then turns to the side, and its shoulders rotate. The next contractions push the shoulders through one at a time. The baby's entire body emerges quickly after that. The newborn cries and takes its first breath. When the umbilical cord turns pale and loses a pulse, health care providers clamp and cut it.

Afterbirth: The final stage is the delivery of the placenta or "afterbirth." Uterine contractions separate the placenta from the wall of the uterus. It passes out through the vagina. Afterbirth is usually rapid (between 5 and 30 minutes), easy, and relatively painless. At this time, health care providers check to make sure that the entire placenta has been expelled. They also repair any tears that may have occurred in or around the perineum. (If a surgical incision was made in the perineum, a procedure called an episiotomy, they stitch it closed.)

If all goes well, the uterus contracts and stays firm. The pressure prevents bleeding from the spot where the placenta was attached. Many women begin breastfeeding their babies very soon after delivery. Breastfeeding stimulates the production and release of the hormone oxytocin, which helps the uterus maintain a healthy firmness. Mothers who do not breastfeed may be given oxytocin to achieve that same purpose.

How Long Does Labor Last?

It varies. Leah Albers at the University of New Mexico studied first births in more than 2,500 women. None of them used pain-relieving drugs or injections of oxytocin to speed up labor. She timed active labor and delivery times (not prelabor). For first births, the active stage averaged nearly 8 hours, but could take as long as 18 hours. Delivery required 54 to 146 minutes.[17]

What Is a Cesarean Delivery, and Why Is It Done?

A cesarean is the birth of a baby by surgical (rather than vaginal) delivery. The origin of the term is a mystery, but the name may have come from Julius Caesar's time (100–44 B.C.). Roman law required the surgical delivery of fetuses from mothers who were dead or dying. The law, historians think, was passed to increase the number of citizens for Caesar's empire.

Today, cesareans, or "C-sections," are performed more often and for less drastic reasons. Two incisions are made: one through the skin of the abdomen and the other through the uterine wall. The cuts may be either vertical (from the navel to the pubic bone, or "midline" incision) or horizontal (from side-to-side just above the pubic hair line, or "bikini" incision). Once the uterus is opened, the baby and placenta are quickly removed, and the uterus and abdomen are stitched closed. A skilled surgeon can often complete a cesarean in less than 15 minutes. Although the procedure is considered safe, complications may include infection, blood clots, or excessive blood loss.

High-risk situations account for one in three cesareans.[18] They are performed when

- the fetus shows signs of distress—for example, the heart rate is slow.
- the head won't fit through the birth canal.
- the umbilical cord is wrapped around the neck or drops through the cervix, which may cut off the oxygen supply to the fetus.

- the mother has high blood pressure, diabetes, or a sexually transmitted disease.
- the birth of more than one fetus (twins, triplets, or more) increases health risks.
- the placenta blocks the cervix or pulls away from the uterine wall too soon.
- the presentation is breech (see next question).

In 2002, 26.1 percent of the babies born in the United States were delivered by cesarean.[19] Many health professionals think that's too many. The U.S. Department of Health and Human Services has called for a 30 percent decrease, and the American College of Obstetricians and Gynecologists agrees. Too many cesareans are done on normal, healthy women and their normal, healthy babies. One third are done because labor slows or stops.[20]

The American College of Nurse Midwives (ACNM) urges women and their doctors to deliver by cesarean only when truly necessary. Avoiding pain, arranging convenient schedules, getting labor "over with," and threatened lawsuits are bad reasons for having a cesarean. "Women risk permanent damage to abdominal and urinary tract organs, longer recovery times, little-or-no-chance for subsequent vaginal birth, and a premature end to their ability to safely bear children," says ACNM former president Mary Ann Shah. "Technology is an alluring panacea for ills, but blind devotion without critical evaluation places women at great risk," she says.[21]

What Is a Breech Birth?

About 96 percent of all babies come head first. Three quarters of them face the mother's back. This is the normal, or vertex, position.

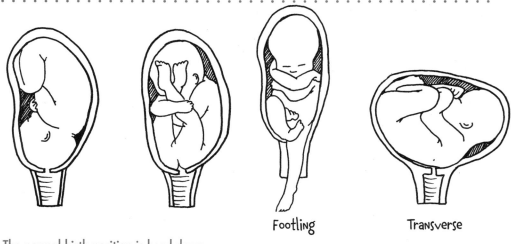

Footling   Transverse

The normal birth position is head down.

By week 36 or 37, most fetuses turn head down into the birth canal spontaneously. This repositioning, called engagement, lightening, or dropping, usually happens two to four weeks before delivery in first-time mothers. In women who have had a previous child, engagement may not occur until labor begins.

If engagement does not occur, the baby is turned with feet or buttocks toward the birth canal. These are called breech positions. They occur in about 4 percent of full-term babies, and more frequently in those born early.[22] Most cases have no apparent cause, but some are associated with placental abnormalities, two or more babies, abnormalities of the uterus, large amounts of amniotic fluid, birth defects, or poor muscle tone in the uterus.

Although breech babies may be born safely through the vagina, many doctors want to reduce the risks for both mother and baby by performing a cesarean. An alternative is to change the position of the fetus, using a procedure called external cephalic version. It is done by manipulating the uterus from the outside and turning the baby into the head-down position. Doctors perform this procedure in a hospital after the 37th week of pregnancy. It's successful nearly two times out of three, but there's a chance that the baby will return to the breech position.[23] Turning heightens the risk of dystocia (labor that fails to progress). The danger of distress to the fetus during delivery also increases. If the fetus becomes entangled in the umbilical cord or the placenta pulls away from the uterine wall too soon, a cesarean delivery is nearly always performed.[24] Researchers at the University of Chicago looked at infant death rates for nearly 400,000 breech babies following vaginal and cesarean deliveries. For such babies, cesarean nearly tripled their chance of survival for the first month of life.[25]

When, Why, and How Do Doctors Induce Labor?

A serious medical condition such as diabetes, high blood pressure, Rh disease, decreased amniotic fluid, or preeclampsia (see Chapter 4) can make continuing a pregnancy past a certain time too hazardous to mother, baby, or both. In such cases, women and their doctors do not want to wait for labor to begin on its own. Even in healthy women, labor may be induced if the pregnancy goes past 40 weeks or if labor stalls or stops.

Any of several steps may be taken to induce labor. The doctor may "strip the membranes." This involves sweeping a finger over the thin membranes that connect the amniotic sac to the wall of the uterus. This procedure triggers the release of prostaglandins, the hormones that ripen the cervix and cause contractions. Breaking the amniotic sac and releasing the fluid may have the same effect.

A laboratory-made version of prostaglandin is often applied to the cervix to start it thinning and opening. Stimulating the nipples releases oxytocin, which speeds up or intensifies uterine contractions. Doctors inject a synthetic form of oxytocin to bring on labor, or to increase the frequency and strength of contractions. Even when labor begins naturally, more than half of all women in the United States get a dose of oxytocin to speed it.[26]

Between 1989 and 2002, the number of labor inductions more than doubled.[27] Some inductions were done to suit the mother's or the physician's schedule. Many physicians frown on this trend, because induction increases risks for both mother and baby. For example, first-time mothers who choose early induction are twice as likely to need a cesarean, compared with those who go into labor naturally. They also face a higher risk of instrument delivery and shoulder dystocia (when the fetal shoulders block the birth canal).[28]

Can a Woman Do Anything to Go into Labor Sooner?

It's a myth that spicy foods, enemas, exercise, fasting, castor oil, herbal teas, and dozens of other do-it-yourself remedies bring on labor. The truth, however, doesn't stop women from believing. Jonathan Schaffir at Ohio State University surveyed 102 pregnant women at a prenatal clinic. He found that two thirds believed walking would start labor. Nearly half thought having sexual intercourse would.[29] Some myths, such as laxatives or starvation to induce labor, can be harmful. For most women, the only way to bring on labor is to wait for it. "For healthy pregnancies, Mother Nature is the best obstetrician," Schaffir says.[30]

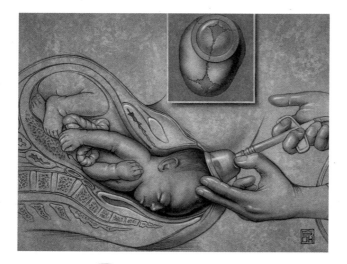

A vacuum suction delivery: The doctor pulls while the mother pushes to help deliver the baby.

Why Do Doctors Use Instruments to Deliver Babies?

Most of the time, they don't. However, an instrument-assisted delivery—using either forceps or vacuum extraction—can reduce risks to mother and baby if there's trouble. Forceps are tonglike devices that fit around the baby's head. Using them, the physician gently pulls the baby from the birth canal. Forceps may also be used to turn the baby's head into a better position for delivery. Vacuum extraction relies on a plastic suction cup placed on the head to achieve the same goal. This procedure is used in about 10 percent of all deliveries.[31]

What Medicines Do Doctors Use to Lessen the Pain of Labor?

Some women neither want nor request pain relief. Some use breathing and relaxation exercises to manage their pain. Some opt to receive narcotic drugs. Narcotics don't affect the source of the pain; they merely change the brain's per-

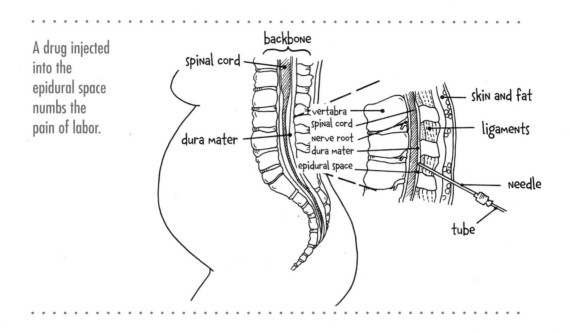

A drug injected into the epidural space numbs the pain of labor.

backbone

spinal cord

vertabra

spinal cord

nerve root

dura mater

epidural space

dura mater

skin and fat

ligaments

needle

tube

ception of it, so it seems less intense. Barbiturate drugs may also be used, not because they block pain but because they reduce fear and anxiety. Because narcotics and barbiturates can slow the fetal heart, breathing, and reflexes, they are not given as delivery draws near.

About half the women in the United States have an epidural block.[32] It does not change the perception of pain. It prevents the pain itself. To perform this procedure, a needle with a tube attached is inserted into the epidural space in the spine. This area is filled with fat and blood vessels. It lies between the bony vertebrae (the small bones of the spine) and the dura mater, a membrane that protects the spinal cord. A numbing drug passes through the tube and needle into the space. The drug bathes the nerves that project out from the lower spine. The drug's action blocks the transmission of pain impulses along the nerves of the pelvic region and the spinal cord. The woman feels the pressure of her contractions but no pain. A spinal block, which is similar to an epidural, is often used for cesarean deliveries. It works faster than an epidural, because the drug goes directly into the fluid that surrounds the spinal cord.

An epidural doesn't make mother or baby groggy, but it can slow labor. Oxytocin may be given to speed things along. Other side effects may include headache, backache, nausea, vomiting, infection, a drop in blood pressure, allergic reactions to the drug, inability to urinate, or failure of heart or breathing—in either mother or fetus. These complications are rare and usually short-lived, but women need to consider them before saying yes to an epidural or spinal block.

How Do Breasts Make Milk?

Each human breast, or mammary gland, is a sweat gland that's modified to produce milk. Visible on the chest are the two nipples—from which milk flows—and an area of darkened, bumpy skin around each one called the areola. The areola contains oil glands that secrete sebum, a lubricant that keeps the nipple supple. Strands of connective tissue called Cooper's ligaments run between the skin and the major muscles of the chest, providing support for the glands. Under the skin of each breast lie 15 to 20 lobes. Each lobe contains many smaller segments called lobules. Embedded in the lobules are grapelike clusters of alveoli. After the

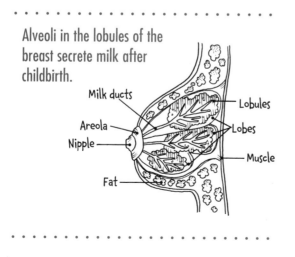

Alveoli in the lobules of the breast secrete milk after childbirth.

Milk ducts

Areola

Nipple

Fat

Lobules

Lobes

Muscle

birth of a child, changing levels of hormones cause the alveoli to begin secreting milk.

The production and ejection of milk from the mammary glands is called lactation. It depends on the hormone prolactin. Prolactin is made throughout pregnancy, but it doesn't cause the mammary glands to start making milk until the levels of estrogen and progesterone fall after delivery. The suckling of a nursing infant stimulates milk production further. It sends nerve impulses to the hypothalamus in the brain. The hypothalamus, in turn, triggers release of the hormone oxytocin from the pituitary gland. Oxytocin causes cells around the alveoli to contract. That action pushes against the alveoli and forces milk from them into the ducts that lead to the nipples.

Is It Possible to Be Pregnant and Not Know It?

Given all the changes that occur in her body, it's hard to believe that any woman would fail to recognize her pregnancy. It happens, however, in a surprising number of cases. German scientists studied hospital records for reports of "denial of pregnancy." They found that denied pregnancies are three times more frequent than triplet births. One in every 475 pregnancies was denied by the woman until after 20 weeks. In one in 2,455 births, the woman did not know she was pregnant until she went into labor. "The common view that denied pregnancies are exotic and rare events is not valid," the researchers concluded.[33] Mild physical symptoms, inexperience or ignorance about pregnancy, inattentiveness to bodily cues, negative feelings about pregnancy, and stress can lead to denial. Women who have been sexually abused as children or feel threatened by pregnancy may fail to recognize their condition.

A Day in the Life of a CNM

· · · · ·

A new baby is like the beginning of all things—wonder, hope, a dream of possibilities.

EDA J. LeSHAN

· · · · ·

"Many years ago, I was in the delivery room and a young woman was about to deliver her first child," says Elizabeth Stein. "One small push and the newborn flew into my arms! I was open mouthed in shock, but the father just said 'good catch.'"

That's one among hundreds of stories Elizabeth has to tell. She is one of America's 7,200 certified nurse midwives (CNMs). They have a nursing degree, plus additional education in women's health, prenatal care, and childbirth. CNMs provide health care to women and their families before, during, and after childbirth. They don't perform surgery, but they may assist, and they deliver babies in homes, birthing centers, and hospitals—calling on medical doctors when emergencies arise.

During their education, CNMs learn much of the same basic science and clinical information as a physician. In their practices, they emphasize what's normal, healthy, and positive about pregnancy. "Our strength is encouraging and empowering the woman and those close to her to decide what is best for them," Elizabeth says. CNMs try to avoid medical technologies and interventions if possible, although safety for mother and baby always comes first. "High touch, low tech," Elizabeth explains.

The work of a CNM is both a career and a commitment. "My day

Elizabeth Stein

starts at 5 or 6 in the morning," she says. "Before I go to the office to see patients, I make rounds in the hospital and attend conferences with other health care providers to review cases. During office hours, I examine patients and answer their questions. I see walk-ins and emergencies. I review and interpret the results that come back from blood and urine tests, mammograms (to check for breast cancer), and sonograms."

Elizabeth usually finishes at the office around 6 P.M., but she's "on call" every third night and every third weekend. She never leaves town, so she is ready whenever a baby decides to come. "I am a 24/7 person. I am wide awake in minutes. All those 3 A.M. calls taught me that! I fall asleep in seconds whenever I lie down. Many times, I have to work 24 to 36 hours straight. Of course, then I collapse." Elizabeth delivers about 80 babies a year. She delivered more than 2,000 in the first 17 years of her practice.

Elizabeth doesn't see pregnant women only. Her patients range in age from 11 to 83. She tries to involve boyfriends, husbands, and fathers-to-be, also. "I encourage fathers to help pregnant women shop, cook, and eat correctly. I suggest they attend childbirth classes together. In labor, I give the papa-to-be specific chores to do, such as giving his partner an ice chip after each contraction, lifting her shoulders, wiping her forehead, or cutting the umbilical cord."

For young people who may be interested in midwifery as a career, Elizabeth suggests getting some information and experience in the teen years. Volunteer for an ambulance corps. Get an EMT (emergency medical technician) license. Work in an emergency room. Work summer, part-time, or as an intern or volunteer in a women's clinic.

"My career as a CNM has taught me so much. It has taught me normalcy, pathology, how women think and react, what they appreciate and what they don't. It has taught me how to speak to women so they hear what I have to say. It has taught me much about the relationships women have with men, and how deeply those relationships affect them."

What's the best thing about being a CNM? "Nothing is more rewarding than feeling this little round head against your hand as a new life enters this world—guided in by me! Hearing that first cry—that is the sound of success!" As for babies that begin life after one small push, Elizabeth laughs as she observes, "The art is in the decision-making. Timing is everything."

CHAPTER THREE

ABOUT PREVENTING AND ENDING PREGNANCY

We are each responsible for our own life—no other person is or even can be.

• OPRAH WINFREY •

Will I Get Pregnant if I Don't Use Contraception?

Within a single year, the chance of pregnancy for a sexually active teen couple not using contraception is 90 percent. In each year, 20 percent of sexually active teen girls get pregnant. Four out of every five of those pregnancies are unplanned.[1]

How Can We Prevent Pregnancy?

Contraception means preventing pregnancy. There are five basic approaches. Only one, sterilization, is permanent. The other four are temporary. They can be stopped when a pregnancy is wanted.

1. **Hormones.** In females, levels of estrogen and progesterone rise and fall over the 28-day menstrual cycle. Hormonal methods of contraception change the pattern. They increase the level of one or both hormones—a signal to the hypothalamus and pituitary gland to limit the production of FSH and LH. With levels of these hormones low, the follicle in the ovary does not develop. An egg is not released. Without a mature egg, pregnancy is impossible. Hormonal methods include pills, injections, skin patches, and vaginal inserts. Hormonal contraceptives are available from doctors, family planning clinics, and health departments.

2. **Barrier.** Barrier methods of contraception include condoms, cervical caps, and diaphragms. They differ in design and materials, but they all do the same thing: prevent sperm cells from reaching the egg. The male condom covers the penis and prevents sperm from entering the vagina. The other barrier methods—including the female condom—cover the cervix and prevent sperm from entering the uterus. A doctor or midwife must fit diaphragms and cervical caps. Female condoms are available in family planning clinics. Male condoms are sold in drugstores and convenience stores. Because sperm can slip around the edges of barriers and because condoms sometimes break, barrier methods are typically used along with a spermicide.

3. **Spermicides.** Sperm-killing chemicals to insert into the vagina can be purchased over the counter. They are available as creams, foams, gels, or suppositories. They must be inserted no longer than one hour before intercourse. Because no spermicide kills all sperm, these preparations are best used along with a barrier method. Unlike condoms, spermicides do not prevent sexually transmitted

diseases. Perhaps because the chemical irritates the lining of the vagina, they may actually increase the risk of transmitting the AIDS virus, HIV. People who are HIV-positive and their sex partners should seek a physician's advice before using a spermicide.

4. **The IUD.** The intrauterine device (IUD) is the world's most popular temporary contraceptive. (The most popular of all is tubal ligation, or permanent sterilization of the female.) An IUD is a small object placed in the uterus by a doctor. It causes changes in the uterine lining that prevent a fertilized egg from implanting. Modern IUDs are made of plastic, copper, or stainless steel. Some contain hormones to

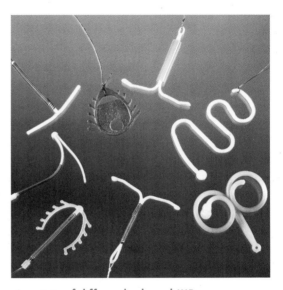

A variety of differently shaped IUDs

increase their effectiveness. They generally are used only in women who have already had a child.

5. **Sterilization** (permanent contraception). Males can have a vasectomy to prevent sperm from being ejaculated in their semen. Females can have a tubal ligation to prevent eggs from entering the fallopian tubes. Although these surgical procedures can sometimes be reversed for people who change their minds, attempted reversals often fail. That's why these procedures must be considered permanent.

Choosing the best contraceptive means answering several questions:

How reliable is it? No method is 100 percent effective, but some get close. Hormonal methods earn a 99+ percent rating in theory. In real life, failure rates can run 10 percent or more, not because the contraceptive fails, but because the user forgets to take a pill, keep a doctor's appointment, or replace a patch on time.[2] Condoms and spermicides are nearly as reliable as hormonal methods, but proper and consistent use is essential. Condoms themselves fail in less than 2 percent of cases, but the failure rate for condom users is 12 percent.[3] The most common error? Neglecting, forgetting, or "not bothering" to use a condom every time, for every single act of sexual intercourse.

How easy is it to use? Female condoms prevent both pregnancy and disease transmission, but some girls and women don't know how to use them. Males may have the same problem, tearing the condom while opening the package or rolling the condom the wrong way. Spermicides used with a condom are effective, but most must be put in the vagina within an hour of intercourse. Put them in too early and they lose their sperm-killing ability.

Are the side effects few, trivial, or short-term? No method is risk free, and some side effects may be more unsettling than others. People who are allergic to latex may develop a rash after using a latex condom. Fortunately, condoms made of polyurethane or synthetic latex are now available. Especially in very young women and in the early months of use, hormonal contraceptives can cause menstrual periods to come more or less often than expected. There may be bleeding between periods, or periods may stop for a while. Although these changes are usually nothing to worry about, some women find them distressing. No side effect is a reason to stop contraception and risk an unwanted pregnancy. Talk to your health care provider to ask if switching methods would be wise.

Are there health benefits not related to contraception? Condoms deliver one health benefit no other method of contraception can claim. They protect against sexually transmitted diseases (STDs). That protection is extremely important for anyone who has an STD or might get one. Any unprotected (noncondom) sex with a new partner risks an STD. Or if there is any chance that your regular sexual partner might have sex with someone else, an STD is possible. (Many girls and women mistakenly believe their male partners are having sex only with them. Males need to be reminded that their girlfriends might be cheating, too.)

For two people who have had medical exams, are sure they are disease free, and are certain they are having sexual intercourse only with each other, "the pill" is a good option. The combined oral contraceptives, or COCs, actually deliver health benefits not related to contraception. They reduce the pain and blood loss of menstrual periods. They can improve complexion in girls with acne. They decrease the risk for cancers of the colon, uterus, and ovary. Pill use cuts the risk of pelvic inflammatory disease (PID) in half. It prevents cysts from forming in the ovaries, and protects bones against osteoporosis, or brittle bone disease.[4] Oral contraceptives do *not*, as was once feared, increase the risk of breast cancer.[5]

How much does it cost? Contraception isn't cheap, but it costs less than an unwanted pregnancy. Financial help is available for those who feel they can't afford contraception. Medicaid and many private insurance plans cover all or part of contraceptive cost. Your local Planned Parenthood clinic or health department can tell you what financial help is available.

How Does "the Pill" Work? In one of two ways. One type of pill, the "combined oral contraceptive" or COC, contains estrogen and progestin, a laboratory-made version of progesterone. This combination of hormones prevents ovulation and makes the lining of the uterus too thin for implantation to occur. Most COCs are taken for 21 days. Menstrual flow begins in the seven days that follow.

The POP or "progestin-only pill" contains no estrogen. POPs work in several ways. They prevent egg release. They also make the mucus of the cervix thick so that sperm can't get through. They slow the movement of the egg through the fallopian tube, and make the lining of the uterus too thin for implantation to occur. POPs are not as well known or as frequently used as COCs. POPs are safer choices for smokers who want to take the pill. Both COCs and POPs should be taken at the same time daily.

Is the Pill Safe? Many commonly used drugs, such as penicillin, are more dangerous than the pill. Pregnancy and childbirth are more dangerous still. Nevertheless, a woman needs to visit a doctor or clinic before she takes contraceptive pills. Her health care provider will explain the risks and possible side effects. New pill users sometimes experience nausea, appetite changes, breast enlargement, vaginal discharge, bleeding between periods, skin discoloration, bloating, or swelling of the legs. If these side effects occur, they are usually mild. They tend to disappear after a few months, as the body adapts to hormonal changes.

More serious is the increased risk of thromboembolism, the blockage of a blood vessel by a clot that breaks free from the place where it formed. Such a blockage can cause a heart attack or a stroke.[6] For that reason, some birth control pills are not recommended for women who smoke or have diabetes, heart disease, liver disease, high blood pressure, a history of blood clots, or a disorder of the immune system called SLE (systemic lupus erythematosus).

Is the Pill the Best Hormonal Method?

"Best" is a judgment that a woman must make after talking with her sexual partner and her doctor. However, the pill is not the only hormonal method available, and many women find injections, vaginal rings, or skin patches more convenient. They work in the same way as the pill, but they do not require daily doses.

Injection. One popular injectable is made from progestin. A health care provider injects it every 12 to14 weeks.

Vaginal Ring. The ring measures about 2 inches (5 cm) across. It contains both estrogen and progestin mixed into the plastic of the ring. Over three week's time, it releases continuous low doses of hormones into the vagina. From there, they pass into the blood. A new ring is inserted each month.

Skin Patch. Patches work like the vaginal ring, except the hormones are absorbed through the skin. Patches block egg release as effectively as other hormonal methods, and may cause slightly fewer complications than pills. A new patch is placed on the skin weekly, anyplace except the breast.

If I Take the Pill Now, Will I Have Trouble Getting Pregnant Later?

No. The hormones in the pill clear from the body in a few days. (The pill is very short-acting. That's why it must be taken daily.) When a woman wishes to become pregnant, she simply stops taking the pill and uses some other method of contraception for three months until her hormonal levels readjust. Then she stops using any contraceptive. The pregnancy rate after stopping the pill is the same as for women who never took it. About 90 percent of women will become pregnant within one year. Rarely, women who had irregular menstrual cycles before taking the pill fail to menstruate after stopping it. This condition may be treated with prescription drugs that trigger egg release and menstruation.

What Is the Right Way to Use a Male Condom?

For first-time condom users, it's a good idea to practice during masturbation. Practice prevents embarrassment or accidents when having sex with a partner. Here are the steps:

- Open the package carefully so you don't tear or rip the condom inside.
- Do not unroll the condom before putting it on.
- If not circumcised, pull your foreskin back.
- Check that the reservoir tip is poking out from the middle of the roll, so you are sure the condom can be unrolled.
- Hold the tip of the condom to squeeze out the air. This leaves some room at the end for the semen that comes out of the penis during ejaculation.

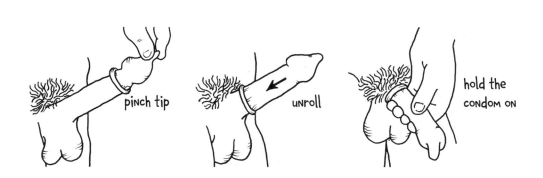

pinch tip

unroll

hold the
condom on

How to use a male condom

- At this point, or earlier, the penis must be erect. You cannot put a condom on a soft penis.
- Before any contact with your partner's mouth, anus, or genitals, place the condom on the end of the penis.
- Unroll the condom down the penis until it covers its entire length.
- After ejaculation and before your erection softens, hold the rim of the condom at the base of the penis.
- Withdraw from contact with your partner.
- Remove the condom from your penis.
- Wrap it in paper or seal it in a plastic bag. Throw it in a covered trashcan or bury it. Do not flush it down the toilet or litter the environment.
- Wash the penis with water and mild soap.

The female condom has some advantages over the more-familiar male version. It allows girls and women to have greater control over sexual situations. Female condoms are made of polyurethane. They are stronger and can be stored longer than male condoms. Because the female condom can be inserted up to eight hours before intercourse, it doesn't "spoil the mood." Like the male condom, it can be used only once.

The female condom offers good protection against both pregnancy and sexually transmitted diseases. The closed end of the female condom covers the cervix and is anchored behind the pubic bone. The outer ring, which is open, rests outside the vagina and covers the vulva. Here's how to use one:

- Find the inner ring of the condom and hold it between your thumb and middle finger.
- Squeeze the ring together and insert as far as possible into the vagina, making sure that the inner ring is past the pubic bone.
- The outer ring should be outside the vagina.
- Make sure the condom has not become twisted. (These steps can be done as much as eight hours ahead of time.)
- Lubricate the penis with a water-based lubricant such as K-Y Jelly. (Do not use Vaseline, body lotion, or any oil-based lubricant.)
- When your partner's penis enters you, hold the plastic sheath to cover your external genitals. (This is important to prevent both pregnancy and sexually transmitted diseases.)
- After intercourse, while standing, squeeze and twist the outer ring to make sure the semen stays inside the condom. Remove it by pulling gently.

- Use only once. Do not flush. Wrap the condom in paper or a plastic bag. Bury it or throw it in a covered garbage can.

It takes practice to learn to insert the female condom properly. New users should practice in private until they become comfortable with the procedure. Also, girls and women must learn to hold the condom in place when a male inserts his penis into the vagina. The penis should thrust inside the condom, not slip between the condom and the vaginal wall. Don't try to use a male condom and a female condom at the same time.

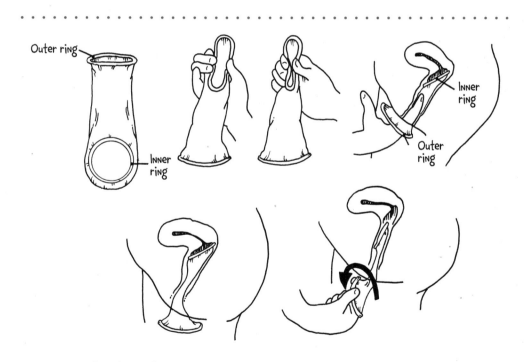

How to use a female condom

What Should We Do if Our Contraceptive Fails?

If you have sex without a condom or if your method fails, contact a health care provider and ask for emergency contraception. Two methods are available. The first is emergency contraceptive pills. They prevent or delay release of an egg. They may also prevent a fertilized egg from implanting in the uterus. The pills are highly effective if taken within three days after intercourse. Also effective is the insertion of a copper-bearing IUD within one week. Emergency contraception is not abortion. Neither method will end an established pregnancy. Emergency contraception doesn't prevent sexually transmitted diseases either. Women and men who have sex without a condom should be tested for STDs.

In some states, emergency pills are available from pharmacists without a prescription. If you are having sex, it's a good idea to get emergency contraceptive pills before an accident happens. That way you'll be ready for the unexpected. You'll be able to prevent pregnancy even on weekends, holidays, and vacations when seeing a doctor might be difficult. To learn more, call 1-800-230-PLAN or 1-888-NOT-2-LATE.

Can We Get the Pill Without Our Parents Knowing?

It depends on where you live. Most states allow minors (usually defined as younger than 18) to obtain contraceptives in confidence, but some states make exceptions. Doctors vary also. Some will not prescribe contraception for young people without notifying parents, even in states where they are allowed to under the law. Your best source of information is your local or state department of public health. Or call Planned Parenthood's contraception hotline at 1-800-230-PLAN.

Will a Pill, Patch, or Injection Make Me Gain Weight? No. Researchers in Ohio tested contraceptive patches against placebo patches. The placebo patches contained no drug, but their users didn't know it. (All women in the study were willing to take the chance of becoming pregnant.) After nine months, weight changes were the same in the two groups.[7] Researchers in New York who studied pills, not patches, drew the same conclusion. Weight gain was not associated with hormone use, but with changes in diet and lifestyle.[8]

How Are Women Sterilized? By a procedure doctors call tubal ligation. The fallopian tubes are tied with a ring or clip or sealed with an electrical current. As a result, eggs cannot travel from the ovaries to the uterus. Unfertilized eggs break down, but the woman continues menstrual periods as normal.

Nearly half of the women who have tubal ligation do so immediately after the birth of a child. The procedure can also be done during or just after a menstrual period. Tubal ligation should be considered a final, irreversible decision. Although reopening the tubes is possible, major surgery is involved and is not always successful. Federal and state laws regulate who can have a tubal ligation and when. It is not an option typically available to women in their teens.

In 2002, an alternative to tubal ligation that requires no surgery became available in some medical centers. Doctors thread a thin, telescope-like hysteroscope through the cervix and uterus and into the fallopian tubes. There, they place a small, soft coil that expands and fills the tube. In the months that follow, scar tissue forms around the coil and blocks the tube. The procedure can be done in a doctor's office, using only local anesthetic, in about 30 minutes. Whether this procedure can replace tubal ligation is a question only time and further research can answer.

How Are Men Sterilized?

Every year, a half million American men get a vasectomy.[9] The typical vasectomy is performed by a surgeon. The operation is simple. It can be done in the doctor's office under local anesthetic. The doctor makes a small incision in the scrotum. Then a short segment is removed from the vas deferens, the tube that carries sperm from the testicles to the urethra. The cut ends of the tube can be heated to seal them, blocked with plastic plugs, or pinched off with a plastic clip. No matter what the method, sperm can no longer pass through the tube, although the fluid portion of semen continues to be ejaculated. Within three weeks, the sperm that were already in the tube are gone. Then a check of a semen sample under the microscope confirms the success of the operation.

A vasectomy does not change a man's sexual desire, performance, or enjoyment. It can, however, fail. In about one in every 1,000 cases, the man's sexual partner becomes pregnant.[10] This happens when the cut ends of the duct reseal themselves, and sperm can travel though the tube once more.

Vasectomy should be considered permanent sterilization. Attempts to reverse the operation—because men change their minds about becoming fathers—are successful only about half the time.[11] Compared with tubal ligation, a vasectomy costs less and risks fewer medical complications, but female sterilization is performed twice as often.

Who Has Abortions, and How Are They Done?

Abortion is the end of a pregnancy by any means other than the birth of a live infant. Most abortions are spontaneous. They happen naturally, without human intervention. They are often called miscarriages (see Chapter 4).

Abortions may also be intentional. They are called elective or induced abortions, and they have been legal in the United States since 1973. Here are some facts:

- In the United States annually, about 900,000 women have an elective abortion.[12]
- One fourth of all pregnancies and one half of all unintended pregnancies end in an elective abortion.[13]
- Eighty percent of the women who have abortions are unmarried. Half are between the ages of 15 and 24.[14]
- One out of 10 college women has had an abortion.
- Two in every five women will have an elective abortion sometime in their lives.[15]

Elective abortions are legal to 24 weeks, but most are done much earlier. More than half are performed before eight weeks, and nearly 90 percent are done before 13 weeks.[16] Several methods are available for early abortions. One frequently used in the first month after a missed period is menstrual extraction, or minisuction. The procedure is usually done in a doctor's office. It does not require a hospital stay. The cervix is opened slightly. A small instrument called a suction cannula is inserted into the uterus. The cannula is attached to a pump. Its vacuum action pulls the embryo and placenta from the uterus. Past seven weeks, a larger cannula and suction source are needed. This method is called vacuum or suction curettage before 13 weeks.

Another procedure, called dilation and curettage (D&C), may be used before the 14th week. The cervix is opened slightly for a D&C, and the contents of the uterus either scraped or suctioned. The D&C procedure is not just for abortions. It is frequently used to treat disorders of the uterine lining. It is performed in the hospital.

Since Food and Drug Administration approval in the fall of 2000, women in the United States have had an alternative to surgical abortion. This alternative, the medical abortion, must be done within the first seven weeks of pregnancy (three weeks after a missed period). Two drugs are used for a medical abortion. The first, mifepristone (also known as RU-486), binds to progesterone receptors. These are sites on the surfaces of cells where progesterone molecules usually attach like keys fitting into locks. With the "keyholes" in the uterine lining blocked, progesterone molecules can't latch on, so they can't do their work in maintaining a pregnancy. The lining of the uterus softens, and the embryo detaches. The placenta breaks away from the uterine wall, the cervix opens, and the uterus contracts. The second drug the woman takes is misoprostol. It is a prostaglandin. Given two days after mifepristone, it triggers strong contractions of the uterus and expulsion of its contents. Within the next two weeks, the doctor examines the woman to make sure the abortion is complete. In up to 95 percent of cases, the procedure succeeds.[17] When it fails, a surgical abortion may be required.

Abortions performed by qualified medical personnel in legal clinics and hospitals are quite safe. The risk of death is less than 1 in 100,000.[18] The risk of dying in childbirth is ten times greater.[19] Complications occur in fewer than 1 in every 1,000 early abortions.[20] They include nausea, vomiting, diarrhea, abdominal pain and cramping, back pain, or a bad-smelling discharge from the vagina. A fever can result from labor-inducing drugs, or it may be a sign of infection. Doctors prescribe drugs to prevent and treat infections, kill pain, and relieve digestive complaints.

Some bleeding after an abortion is normal. Hemorrhage, which is bleeding heavy enough to require a blood transfusion, is possible, but rare. So is the possibility of puncturing or tearing the uterus, cervix, bowel, or bladder with a surgical instrument. In such cases, additional surgeries may be needed to repair the damage. Despite what you may have heard, there is no link between abortion and an increased risk of breast cancer.[21]

Emotional or psychological problems sometimes develop. Wendy J. Lewis of the University of Western Ontario studied them. "The vast majority of women undergoing the legal abortion of an unwanted pregnancy during the first trimester do not suffer adverse effects, at least in the short-term," she says. "A small minority of women, however, do appear to experience adjustment difficulties."[22] Factors for greater risk of psychological troubles include:

- age younger than 19
- unmarried with no children
- anti-abortion religious beliefs
- psychiatric illness

- difficulty with the decision to have an abortion
- external pressure to have an abortion
- the meaningfulness of the pregnancy (that is, whether the pregnancy was intentional)
- abortion for reasons of birth defects in the fetus
- abortion during the second trimester
- self-blame for the pregnancy
- expectation of an inability to cope
- lack of support from friends and family.

Does Abortion Affect Future Pregnancies?

Maybe. Researchers at the Institute of Planned Parenthood Research examined the medical records of more than 60,000 women in Denmark. They found that women who had one previous abortion faced a 17 percent increase in their risk of retained placenta (a placenta that does not deliver within 30 minutes after fetal delivery) in their next pregnancy. Those who had two or more abortions increased their risk by 68 percent.[23] The authors think that trauma to the uterine lining could be the reason, but more research is needed.

Abortion Is Legal, But Is It Right?

In the recent history of the United States, no other moral question has sparked more controversy than this one. Although abortion became legal in the United States in 1973, "pro-choice" and "pro-life" advocates in virtually every state continue to fight for their views in the media, the courts, and the legislatures. Laws vary among states and change often. More than half the states require minors to inform their parents, or gain their consent, before having an abortion. Some states require a waiting period of up to 48 hours.[24] While 43 states and the District of Columbia mandate that only physicians can perform abortions, doctors are not required to perform them, and many choose not to.[25]

Laws cannot answer the moral question of whether abortion is right or wrong. Science and medicine can't answer the question either. That answer must come from deep inside the woman herself—where her conscience, religious faith, and philosophy of life dwell. Physician Jeffrey K. Pearson writes:

> Abortion is not a medical issue *per se*. It's a relatively simple, usually uncomplicated procedure. As physicians, we can only educate our patients about the pros and cons of any medical option. Ultimately, it's a woman's right to decide. Our patients make the decisions that are best for them based on their life experiences. . . . What works for one patient will not necessarily work for another. We have to respect their decisions regardless of our own personal beliefs.[26]

The Search for the Male Contraceptive Pill

· · · · ·

*The contraceptive pill of today is not the same as it was
yesterday, neither will it be the same in the future.*

Lara V. Marks

· · · · ·

The year was 1960. The pill was Enovid. It changed the world.

For the first time in history, pregnancy could be prevented with almost total certainty. Women rushed to get and use the pill. Between 1960 and 1970, the birthrate in the United States dropped by half.[27]

Since then, with the exception of vasectomies and the male condom, preventing pregnancy has been mostly "woman's work." Some women—and some scientists—would like to change that. How? By developing a contraceptive pill for males. Three approaches are being explored in research laboratories and clinical trials. They are (1) to suppress sperm production with hormones; (2) to suppress sperm production without hormones; or (3) to inhibit the fertilizing ability of sperm.

The first approach has received the most attention, with studies of the primary male hormone, testosterone. An elevated testosterone level in the blood signals the pituitary gland to slow the release of FSH and LH. Both are necessary for sperm development. So, in theory, an extra dose of testosterone should interfere with sperm production. It works, but not without side effects. One potentially serious one is a decline in HDL molecules. These are the "good cholesterol" molecules in the blood that protect against heart attacks.

Another idea is to use hormones that stop sperm from developing, but that also reduce testosterone levels.

"Don't worry, ladies, I'm on the pill."

"The Pill" for Men

This mock advertisement was part of a *Time* magazine article called "If Men Took the Pill . . ."

Less testosterone can mean loss of muscle mass, acne, or decreased interest in sex—side effects most men object to. The solution is "add-back" therapy, or giving a "make-up-the-difference" dose of testosterone. Christina Wang and her team at Harbor–UCLA Medical Center report good results with this approach. In one trial, men who got implants of levonorgestrel (a hormone often used in female contraceptives) plus testosterone injections had their sperm production suppressed to very low levels without undesirable side effects.[28]

While hormonal methods may eventually prove as effective for men as for women, some scientists think nonhormonal methods may work out as well or better. One nonhormonal drug that suppresses sperm production is gossypol. This derivative of cottonseed oil was widely tested in

China in the 1970s. The drug worked as an effective contraceptive. It could be taken easily and it did not interfere with testosterone production. It turned out, however, to have some serious side effects. It produced permanent sterility in some who used it. It interfered with kidney function in some, too. In 1986, concern about side effects ended the Chinese research, but some scientists think lower doses of gossypol, or an analogue (chemically similar compound) might eventually prove a safe and reliable contraceptive.

The third approach does not prevent sperm from being formed, but interferes with their fertilizing ability. The drug mifepristone, or RU-486, the medical abortion drug for women, acts on the outer membrane of sperm cells. It interferes with calcium use and stops sperm from swimming properly. Another drug, nifedipine, is often prescribed to combat high blood pressure and migraine headaches. It blocks the release from sperm cells of the enzymes that penetrate the outer coating of the egg cell, thus preventing fertilization.

Another enzyme-blocking system has been investigated at Harvard University. Studying mice, David Clapham and his team found a gene that controls the flow of ions (charged atoms) of calcium. The gene is active only in the tails of sperm. Without it, sperm are poor swimmers and cannot perform the whiplash motion needed to penetrate an egg.[29] If a calcium-blocking drug could be developed, it might turn healthy sperm into such lazy swimmers that either men or women could use it to prevent pregnancy.

Another idea is to vaccinate a man against his own sperm. It has worked in guinea pigs. When given a dose of proteins from sperm, the animals' blood made antibodies that attacked that protein—just as they would an invading microorganism. Sperm cells with antibodies attached cannot fertilize an egg.

Which of these approaches will change the world as Enovid did remains to be seen. Meanwhile, work continues. "Our goal," says Christina Wang, "is a long-acting . . . user-friendly contraceptive."[30]

CHAPTER FOUR

20 QUESTIONS

ABOUT WHEN THINGS GO WRONG

Not all the seeds you plant in your garden grow.
• SHELDON M. CHERRY •

I Have Trouble with My Menstrual Periods. What's Happening?

The answer depends on many factors: your symptoms, age, health history, and more. Some problems are minor and will get better in time. Others require medical help. Some of the more common reasons for seeing a doctor include:

Heavy or prolonged bleeding (menorrhagia): Bleeding a lot—or for more than seven days a cycle—can result from an inherited bleeding disorder, but it can have many other causes. Most often in young women, the cause is a hormone imbalance, and doctors often prescribe the pill to correct it. Some nonhormonal drugs may also lessen the bleeding. Sometimes, heavy bleeding results from polyps or fibroids (noncancerous growths) in the uterus. To spot them, physicians insert

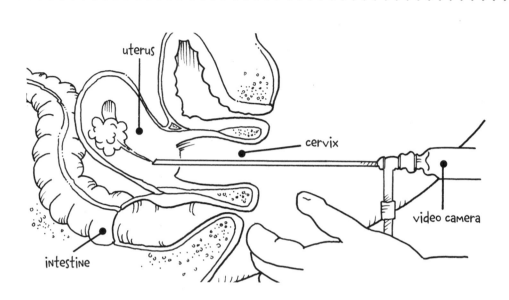

A hysteroscope (above) is an ultrathin telescope that allows the doctor to see inside the uterus. The image below shows uterine fibroids as seen through the hysteroscope.

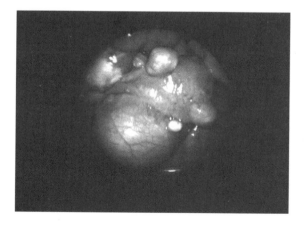

through the cervix an instrument called a hysteroscope. With it, they can examine the inside of the uterus. They may find that the lining has grown too thick, a condition called hyperplasia. Freezing or scraping the uterine lining can treat severe cases.

Pain (dysmenorrhea): If you have painful periods, you're not alone. In one study, nearly three in every four young women who visited a family planning clinic complained of menstrual pain. One quarter said the pain was severe enough to interfere with their normal activities.[1] For many women, rest, a heating pad, soothing herbal teas, and over-the-counter medications such as Midol see them through. For others, doctors prescribe drugs to reduce the thickness of the uterine lining or curb the production of the prostaglandins that provoke painful contractions of the uterus.

Absence of menstrual periods (amenorrhea): If a girl has not had her first period by age 16, or within two years after her breasts develop, a doctor may diagnose primary amenorrhea. Possible causes include developmental problems (absence of a uterus), shifts in hormone balance, and diseases of the ovary or thyroid gland. Girls who eat too little or exercise excessively may disrupt their natural hormone cycles enough to stop their periods. This risks not only reproductive functions, but the health of bones as well. In women who previously have had menstrual periods and are not pregnant or entering menopause (when menstruation stops for good around age 50), the absence of periods is called secondary amenorrhea. Doctors use many different means to diagnose and treat amenorrhea.

Irregular or long cycles (oligomenorrhea): When the interval between periods exceeds 35 days, doctors may diagnose oligomenorrhea. Many women with this condition do not release an egg from their ovaries. The reason may be small cysts that form in the ovaries, causing an abnormal increase in the minute amount of male hormone normally made there. Stress, illness, tumors, or poor diet can cause it, too. The condition is common among teenagers and usually resolves on its own, without treatment. If treatment is needed, the pill usually corrects the hormonal imbalance.

By the way, if you smoke, tobacco may be the cause of your problems. Cigarette smoking causes painful menstruation, irregular periods, and early menopause. Smoking increases the risk of infection in the fallopian tubes, perhaps because tobacco damages the immune system's ability to fight off infections. In pregnant women, smoking increases the risk of miscarriage, rupture of the membrane sacs before labor begins, separation of the placenta from the uterus, high blood pressure, abnormal location of the placenta, and serious bleeding during labor.

What is Pelvic Inflammatory Disease?

Pelvic inflammatory disease (PID) is any infection of the uterus, fallopian tubes, or ovaries. Although PID can occur with no symptoms at all, pain in the lower abdomen and an abnormal discharge from the vagina are often the first signs. Other symptoms may include fever, painful intercourse, and irregular bleeding. PID probably begins as an untreated STD such as chlamydia or gonorrhea. Antibiotics clear the infection in 90 percent of cases. A blockage of a fallopian tube or chronic pain remains in about a third of all cases.[2]

Some one million women are treated for PID in the United States each year. The infection rate is highest among teenagers. One in every seven women will be treated at some time in her life. More than 100,000 women become infertile each year because of PID.[3]

(Infertility is the inability to become pregnant or to sustain a pregnancy. Read more about it in Chapter Five.)

What Is Endometriosis?

Endometriosis is the presence of uterine lining tissue in places outside the uterus. It is a common cause of infertility. Up to 10 percent of women of childbearing age have endometriosis, many of them without symptoms.[4] If symptoms are present, the first is often pelvic pain that occurs around the time of menstruation. Endometriosis worsens when the estrogen level is high and improves when it is low. Little is known about how it begins or why estrogen makes it worse. Oral contraceptive pills suppress ovulation, and the progesterone in them can diminish symptoms. Other prescription drugs are available.

What Kinds of Cancers Develop in the Reproductive System?

Cancer is uncontrolled cell growth. Cells that shouldn't divide do, forming a mass of cells or a tumor. Tumors can be benign (slow-growing and usually harmless) or malignant (fast-growing and likely to spread). Malignant tumors can invade and destroy nearby healthy tissues and organs. Cancer cells can also spread to other parts of the body and form new tumors. The process of spread is called metastasis. Cancer is rare in young people; risks increase in both men and women as they grow older.

Cancer can occur in any part of the body, including the organs of the reproductive system. In males, they include:

Prostate. A tumor causes the gland to swell, making urination frequent and difficult. Since these same symptoms are common in many healthy men over 65 (in whom nearly three in four prostate cancers are found), prostate cancer was difficult to diagnose until a test for the protein PSA (prostate specific antigen) was developed.[5] A high level suggests a possible cancer in the prostate. The test led to a rapid rise in diagnoses of prostate cancer in the 1990s. More than 190,000 new cases were identified in the United States in 2004.

Testicles and penis. Compared with prostate cancer, cancers of the penis or testicles are rare. Combined, they accounted for fewer than 9,000 new cases in 2004. The kind of cancer that develops in the penis depends on the cells that become cancerous. About 95 percent develop from skin cells, usually on the foreskin of uncircumcised men or on the

. . . .

TESTICULAR SELF-EXAM

1) Take a warm bath or shower. The heat relaxes the scrotum.
2) Look in the mirror. Look for lumps or swelling. Don't worry if one testicle is bigger than the other. That's normal.
3) Roll each testicle between your thumb and fingers.
4) Find the epididymis. Don't confuse it with a lump.
5) Report any lump, tenderness, hardness, discharge, or pain to your health care provider.

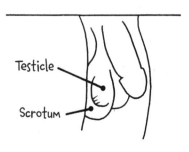

Testicle

Scrotum

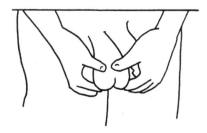

. . . .

glans. Most of these tumors grow slowly. When detected early, they can usually be cured with few complications. Nearly half of all testicular cancers develop from the sperm-producing cells. They occur mostly in older men. In younger men, the cancers are more likely to arise in non–sperm-producing cells. Regular self-examinations allow early detection.

Cancers that affect the reproductive organs of females include:

Breast. More than 215,000 new cases of breast cancer were diagnosed in 2004, and about 40,000 individuals (400 of them men) died of breast cancer that year. Some breast cancers are found during a breast self-examination or a routine physical exam performed by a health care provider. Others are found with a mammogram, or X-ray examination of the breast. A lump, infection, thickening, skin irritation, or dimple may indicate a change in breast tissue. Breast pain is rarely a symptom. The American Cancer Society recommends a mammogram every year beginning at age 40. Younger women should examine their own breasts monthly and have a breast examination by a health care professional at least every three years.[6]

Some risk factors for breast cancer, such as a family history of the disease, are beyond an individual's control. Everyone, however, can reduce personal risk by eating fewer fatty foods, limiting alcohol intake, and maintaining a healthy body weight. Another do-it-yourself preventive is regular exercise. In one study, an hour a day of recreational activity reduced breast cancer risk by 18 percent.[7]

Cervix. About 10,000 new cases of cervical cancer occur annually. Since the 1960s, the death rate from cervical cancer has fallen by 70 to 80 percent. The main reason is the Pap test. It is a screening test. (Screening means testing everyone and spotting those suspicious cases in need of closer examination.) Every woman who is sexually active or age 18 or older should get one yearly. To perform the test, a health

BREAST SELF-EXAM

LOOK

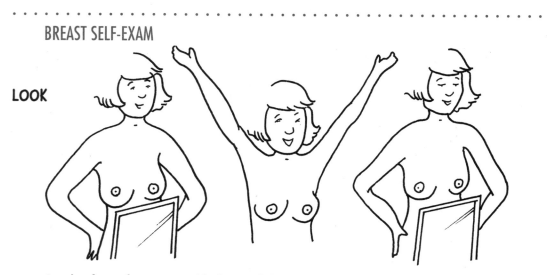

Stand in front of a mirror and look at each breast. Notice the size, shape, and color of your breasts and nipples, and be alert to changes.

FEEL

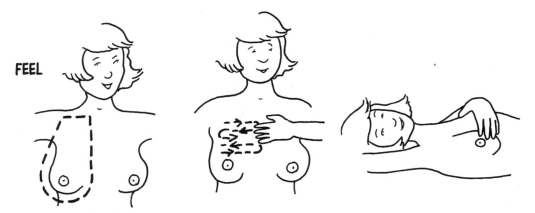

Start your breast self-exam just below your collarbone. With the tips of your fingers, feel the breast and surrounding tissue. Move your fingers in a sweeping or circular pattern, using firm pressure. After examining your other breast the same way, lie down and repeat the exam. Lying down flattens the breast. In both positions, be alert to new or larger bumps or masses.

care provider swabs a sample of cells from the cervix. The cells are viewed through a microscope in search of possibly cancerous changes. Infection with the sexually transmitted disease HPV (human papillomavirus) greatly increases the risk of cervical cancer, but it is highly treatable if diagnosed early.

Uterus. Cancers of the uterus, usually the uterine lining, are found in more than 40,000 women each year, most of them middle-aged or older. The first symptom may be bleeding between menstrual periods or bleeding after menopause. Pregnancy and the use of oral contraceptives while young reduce the risk of uterine cancer in later life. Diagnosis begins with an ultrasound scan that measures the thickness of the uterine lining. If it appears abnormal, a biopsy is performed. A biopsy is a microscopic examination of cells.

Ovary. The first symptom of ovarian cancer is often swelling of the abdomen. It happens because fluid accumulates there. Women who have never had children face a greater risk. Ovarian cancer can be found during routine pelvic examination. There is no screening test for ovarian cancer, but in suspicious cases a sonogram can reveal growths that require biopsy. More than 25,000 new cases are diagnosed annually, and more than 16,000 women lose their lives to the disease each year. Since 1991, the number of new cases of ovarian cancer has been declining. The progress is the result of earlier diagnosis and improved treatments.

Like other cancers, cancers of the reproductive system can be treated in one or more of the following ways:

Hormone therapy. In men, hormone therapy shuts down testosterone, which is often responsible for making a prostate tumor grow. It is commonly given for two months before and two months during radiation therapy.[8] A variation on hormone treatment is the anticancer drug tamoxifen. It interferes with estrogen activity. It is prescribed for both women and men who have breast cancer.

Chemotherapy, or drugs that kill cancer cells. Most work in one of two ways: Either they block the manufacture of DNA in the nucleus of tumor cells, or they interfere with cell division. Most anticancer drugs are given by injection. A few are taken by mouth.

Radiation, or the use of high-energy rays and particles to kill tumor cells or slow their growth. Radiation is often effective against small tumors. Sometimes it is delivered from machines that focus a beam on the tumor. For some cancers, rods or pellets of radioactive material may be implanted in or near the tumor. Implants deliver a continuous dose of radiation over time.

Surgery, or the removal of a tumor, all or in part. Surgeons treat breast cancer with a lumpectomy (removal of the tumor) or a radical mastectomy (removal of the breast and the lymph nodes under the arm). The uterus and ovary may be removed in women, as may the prostate gland in men. Surgery is often combined with hormones, radiation, or chemotherapy.

Immunotherapy, or the use of the body's own immune defenses to destroy tumor cells. Most such therapies are experimental. The idea is to inject substances into the blood that mimic or enhance the body's defenses against disease-causing invaders, such as viruses or bacteria. In one such research project, scientists at the University of Connecticut are trying to develop a vaccine against breast cancer. Using molecules called heat-shock proteins, they hope to trigger an attack of the immune system's T cells on tumors.[9]

What Is an Ectopic Pregnancy?

An ectopic pregnancy is the implantation of a fertilized egg outside the uterus. Nearly all occur in a fallopian tube. About one in 50 pregnancies is ectopic.[10] Most abort naturally. Those that don't must be treated. The embryo cannot develop normally, and the continuation of the pregnancy risks rupture, severe bleeding, and death to the mother. In some cases, drugs can be prescribed to stop the growth of the tissue and allow the body to absorb it over time. In other instances, surgery is required.

A tool called a laparoscope is used to locate an ectopic pregnancy. This slender, light-transmitting rod is inserted through a small incision in the abdomen. It lets a physician see and examine the internal organs. If the pregnancy is early and the tube is not ruptured, the ectopic tissue may be removed using the laparoscope. A larger incision in the abdomen, or laparotomy, may be needed if the ectopic mass is large or blood loss is life-threatening to the woman. If the fallopian tube is not damaged, or if it can be repaired, women who have had an ectopic pregnancy stand a good chance of a normal pregnancy in the future.

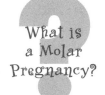
What is a Molar Pregnancy?

A molar pregnancy, also called gestational trophoblastic disease (GTD), is an abnormality of the placenta. There are two types, complete and partial. A complete molar pregnancy has only placental parts, but no embryo. It happens when a sperm cell fertilizes an egg in which the nucleus is inactive or missing. Because the placenta grows and produces hCG, a pregnancy test is positive. A partial molar pregnancy occurs when two sperm cells fertilize a single egg cell. With too many chromosomes, the embryo soon dies in the uterus, but the placenta may remain.

Molar pregnancies are usually diagnosed with an ultrasound examination, or sonogram. The test shows the placenta developing as a mass of cysts resembling a bunch of grapes. Treatment is a procedure called dilation and curettage (D&C). The cervix is expanded, and the contents of the uterus are removed by suction and scraping. In the United States, about 1 out of every 1,000 pregnancies is molar.[11] Women who have a molar pregnancy must be followed closely after treatment, because many complications can develop.

Why Do Women Need the Rubella Vaccine Before Pregnancy?

The rubella virus (German measles) won't make a pregnant woman very sick, but it can blind, cripple, or kill her unborn child. The critical period is the first trimester, when the virus can cause miscarriage or damage the fetus. Rubella can cause deafness, heart abnormalities, mental retardation, or cerebral palsy. Some babies affected by rubella are born underweight. They may have diarrhea, pneumonia, meningitis (inflammation around the brain), anemia, or trouble feeding. The liver and spleen may be enlarged. These children also face an increased risk of diabetes.

Rubella syndrome is totally preventable. While most women today are immune to rubella—because they had the disease or were vaccinated in childhood—2 in every 10 are not.[12] In 1969, a vaccine that prevents rubella became available. A simple blood test can determine whether the antibody that attacks the rubella virus is present in a woman's blood. If it isn't, she can be safely vaccinated three months before she becomes pregnant.

What Symptoms Signal Trouble During Pregnancy?

Eight major danger signs are vaginal bleeding, swelling of the face or fingers, blurry vision, severe or continuous headache, constant or severe pain in the abdomen, persistent vomiting, fever, and fluid discharge from the vagina. Any one of these symptoms raises a red flag that says, "Contact a health care provider or hospital immediately."

What Are Some Medical Problems Possible During Pregnancy?

This list is long. It includes:

Placental abruption, or the detachment of the placenta from the uterus before the fetus is delivered. A slight separation may cause no problems, but a large separation poses a serious threat to the fetus. In such cases, early delivery, usually by cesarean, is the preferred treatment.

Placenta previa, or the blockage of the cervical opening by the placenta. The fetus cannot pass into the birth canal because the placenta blocks it. It happens because the fertilized egg implants too low in the uterus. The block may be partial or complete. Often, placenta previa corrects itself during pregnancy. The uterus grows and pulls the placenta upward into a more normal position. When it does not, doctors perform a cesarean.

Prolapsed cord, or the descent of the umbilical cord through the birth canal before the fetus. This threatens the fetus, because contractions of the uterus block its blood supply. Unless vaginal birth is immediate, delivery by cesarean is necessary.

Premature rupture of the membranes, or breaking of the amniotic sac before labor begins. If this happens months before the due date, doctors usually prescribe bed rest as they watch the pregnancy closely. If it happens at 37 weeks or later, most physicians recommend inducing labor.

Fetal distress, or slowed heartbeat or absence of movement in a fetus. The most common cause is a lack of oxygen during labor or delivery. An immediate delivery by cesarean is usually performed in such cases.

What Is Preeclampsia?

Preeclampsia is a set of symptoms that occur together, usually in the last months of pregnancy. They are high blood pressure, protein in the urine, and swelling of the face and hands. (Commonly in pregnancy, an accumulation of fluid causes swelling of hands and feet. Extra blood production and pressure from the growing uterus on the major vein to the heart slow circulation and cause swelling. Alone, swelling is not a sign of preeclampsia.)

The cause of preeclampsia is unknown, but it may have something to do with poor blood flow to the placenta. One theory suggests that lessened flow triggers a release of oxygen compounds into the blood. These, in turn, interfere with the release of nitric oxide, a natural product that keeps blood vessels relaxed and blood pressure normal.

If accompanied by seizures or coma, the condition is called eclampsia. Its other symptoms include headache, nausea, vomiting, confusion, and visual disturbances resulting from swelling in the brain. Although eclampsia threatens fewer than 2 in every 1,000 pregnancies, it is second only to hemorrhage as a cause of maternal death in the United States.[13]

The risk of eclampsia doubles in women younger than 20, compared with older mothers.[14] Other risk factors include a family history of the disorder, high blood pressure before pregnancy, kidney disease, carrying more than one fetus, poverty, poor nutrition, and obesity. Good prenatal care is the best prevention. In fact, experts say good medical care for all pregnant women could cut the death rate from eclampsia in half.[15]

What Is a Miscarriage?

The unintended loss of a pregnancy before 20 weeks is a spontaneous abortion, or miscarriage. One third of recognized pregnancies end this way. Another one fourth abort naturally before a woman misses a menstrual period or realizes she is pregnant. More than half result from abnormalities of the embryo's chromosomes.[16]

Most early miscarriages happen because the embryo is not growing or developing properly. Miscarriages in the second trimester may arise from problems with the uterus or cervix. Women with untreated diabetes face a greater risk of miscarriage. So do those with vaginal or uterine infections or hormonal disorders. Smoking or drinking alcohol increases risks, as do some toxins in the environment. Exercise, sexual intercourse, morning sickness, and frightening experiences do not cause miscarriage.

Some miscarriages can be prevented with proper medical care, but most cannot. Potential parents who experience a miscarriage often grieve and blame themselves. They need the support of friends and family. Counseling can often help them come to terms with their loss.

ENVIRONMENTAL HAZARDS MAY INCREASE THE RISK OF MISCARRIAGE [17]			
CONFIRMED	**SUSPECTED**	**UNKNOWN**	**DOUBTFUL OR DISPUTED**
Ionizing radiation (such as radioactive materials in a nuclear power plant)	Fever	Pesticides	Diagnostic X-rays
Organic solvents (e.g., toluene in paint)	Hyperthermia (e.g., hot tubs)	Herbicides	Air travel
Alcohol	Phthalates (plastics)		Microwave ovens
Mercury			Electromagnetic fields
Lead			Video display monitors
Cigarette smoking			Aspartame (artificial sweetener)
			Chocolate
			Bovine growth hormone used in milk production
			Phytoestrogens (hormone-like compounds in plants)
			Hair dyes
			Nail polish

What Is Stillbirth?

The death of a fetus after 20 weeks but before birth. Labor and delivery may proceed normally, but the fetus is born dead. Stillbirths are mainly caused by genetic or congenital defects, problems with the umbilical cord or placenta, or a medical condition in the mother.

What Is Rh Disease?

Human blood contains many proteins that have different letter names. The most familiar are the proteins A and B that determine the A, B, AB, and O blood groups. Another blood protein is called Rh. A person who is Rh+ (read R H positive) has the protein. A person who is Rh– (read R H negative) does not. In most cases, the presence or absence of the Rh protein has no effect on health. If, however, an Rh– woman is carrying an Rh+ fetus, her blood can make antibodies that will attack the Rh protein. The first pregnancy is usually fine, but during labor and delivery, some fetal blood may leak through the placenta and enter the mother's bloodstream. If that happens, her blood may begin manufacturing anti-Rh antibodies. In the next pregnancy, her antibodies may attack and destroy red blood cells in the fetal blood.

A substance called RhoGAM (Rh immunoglobulin) is given to Rh– mothers who carry Rh+ babies. RhoGAM stops the mother's body from making anti-Rh antibodies. It is often given around 28 weeks of pregnancy and again after an Rh+ baby is born. It is also given at the time of miscarriage, abortion, amniocentesis, ectopic pregnancy, or whenever an Rh– mother has bleeding in the last three months of pregnancy.

What Are the Most Common Birth Defects?

Each year in the United States, about 4 percent of the babies born live have a birth defect of some kind. That's 150,000 newborns every year.[18] Some birth defects are correctable, and survival has improved greatly in recent years. For example, the number of babies dying from defects in muscles, bones, or digestive organs has declined dramatically since 1970, largely because of better surgical treatments.[19]

Other defects threaten a newborn's survival and cause 20 percent of all infant deaths.[20] Number one on the list are abnormalities of the heart and circulatory system. The most common of them is hypoplastic left heart syndrome, or HLHS.[21] It is the failure of the left side of the heart to develop normally. The heart's main pumping chamber, the left ventricle, may be absent or small. The lower part of the aorta, the major artery that carries blood from the heart to the body, may be missing or misshapen, as may one or more heart valves. A series of

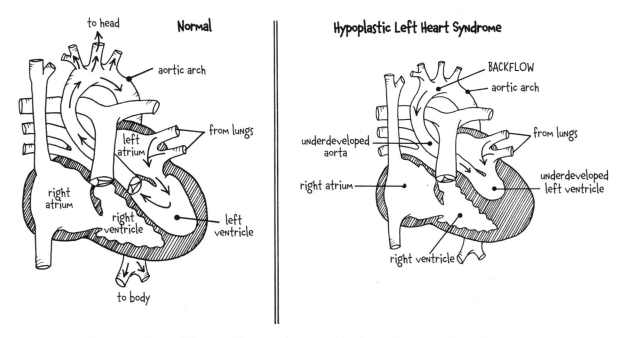

In the normal heart (left), the left ventricle pumps blood into the aorta. From there it goes to the head and body. But if the left ventricle and aorta are underdeveloped (right), the blood does not circulate properly. It may even flow back into the heart.

heart operations can sometimes correct the defects. In severe cases, hope lies in a heart transplant.

Another major category of birth defects includes abnormalities of the spine and brain, together known as the neural tube defects (NTDs). Normally, in the fifth and sixth weeks of pregnancy, the embryo's notochord grows longer. Parallel folds of tissue rise around it, forming a valley, the neural groove. The edges of the folds grow together across the groove and fuse, forming the neural tube. The neural tube develops into the brain and spinal cord. If anything goes wrong with this process, the result is a neural tube defect.

The neural tube closes early in pregnancy. If anything goes wrong with this process, the fetus develops a neural tube defect. (1) Two folds of ectoderm rise along the embryo's back. These ridges are the neural folds. (2) A depression, the neural groove, forms between the neural folds. (3) The folds move closer together, forming the neural crest. (4) The edges of the folds grow together across the groove and fuse, forming the neural tube. (5) Spinal nerves begin to develop from the neural crest.

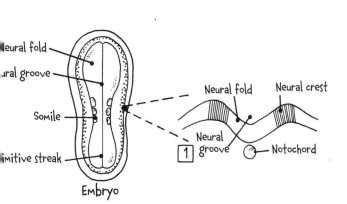

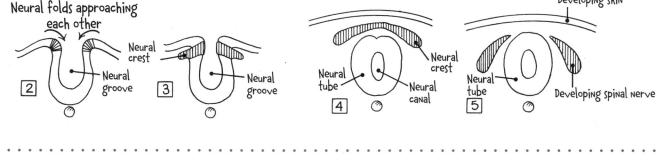

NTDs can take any of several forms. The most common is spina bifida, the failure of the spine to close properly. Spina bifida affects about 1 out of every 1,000 newborns in the United States.[22] In the worst cases, the spinal cord protrudes through the back, protected only by skin or a thin membrane. Back surgery performed within hours after birth reduces the risk of infection and protects the spinal cord against additional damage. However, some paralysis is unavoidable, and further surgeries are often needed. Many children born with spina bifida also have hydrocephalus, the accumulation of fluid in the brain. A surgical procedure called shunting drains fluid from the skull into the abdomen. Many NTD cases can be prevented with good nutrition. (Learn more on page 118.)

Does Pollution Cause Birth Defects?

Some experts say yes. For example, researchers at the University of California at Los Angeles examined birth records in four southern California counties. Where the air contained the most carbon monoxide (a product of automobile engines), the risk of certain heart defects ran highest. The same held true for ozone, another air-polluting gas.[23]

Sometimes pollution comes from unexpected sources. In 2000, a panel of the National Institutes of Health reviewed nearly 1,000 research studies on the health effects of phthalates (pronounced *thalates*). Phthalates are chemicals put into plastics to make soft wraps and bags. The panel concluded that one phthalate, DEHP, can leach out of plastic food packages and be ingested, breathed in, or absorbed through the skin. Fat-digesting enzymes in the intestine convert DEHP to another compound, MEHP, which can harm the developing reproductive tract in male fetuses.[24]

While most people realize that radiation and chemicals pose a hazard to women, fewer understand that they also threaten men. Breathing or ingesting lead, for example, reduces the number of sperm. It may alter sexual hormones and impede the sexual response in men. Radiation exposure can have the same effect, causing sterility in the man or birth defects in his children. The effects of radiation and chemicals depend on the amount of exposure, the time period exposed, the nature of the substance, and the person's inherited susceptibility or resistance.

Today, four million chemical substances are in use. Few of them have been researched. Their reproductive consequences are largely unknown.[25]

Can Birth Defects Be Prevented?

Birth defects arise from a variety of causes: defects in the egg or sperm; genetic or chromosomal abnormalities in either parent; the mother's exposure to harmful drugs or radiation during her pregnancy; the mother's body being too young to properly nourish the fetus; premature birth; or lack of oxygen to the baby during birth. In about 70 percent of cases, however, the cause is unknown.[26]

Nonetheless, we know how to prevent many birth defects. One highly preventable cause of birth defects is obesity in the mother. It increases the risk of a brain, heart, or digestive system defect in an infant by some 30 to 40 percent.[27] Overweight or obesity in the mother also increases the risk of newborn death. Another totally preventable defect is fetal alcohol syndrome.

Many neural tube defects can be prevented by the simplest of all medicines: food! Folic acid is a B vitamin in food that cells need when making DNA, the master molecule that controls cell development. Good sources of folate (the natural form of folic acid) include fortified breakfast cereals, beans, black-eyed peas, cantaloupe, orange juice, and dark-green, leafy vegetables such as turnip greens. Women in their childbearing years need at least 400 micrograms (0.4 milligram) of folic acid daily. The requirement increases to 800 to 1,000 micrograms (0.8–1.0 milligram) daily during pregnancy.

Concerned that too many young women weren't getting enough folic acid, the U.S. Food and Drug Administration in 1998 ordered the addition of folic acid to breads and cereals. That step increased folic acid in the average American diet by 100 micrograms a day. In the years that followed, the rate of two specific NTDs fell by 19 percent.[28] Experts think folic acid supplements could reduce all neural tube defects by as much as 75 percent.[29] Most daily multivitamin pills contain the recommended amount.

Can Sexually Transmitted Diseases (STDs) Harm a Fetus?

Yes, and women should be treated for them before pregnancy or as soon as possible, if they are already pregnant. During pregnancy and at every other time, the best treatment is prevention. That means not having sex or using a condom during every sexual act.

The table on the facing page names some of the microorganisms that cause STDs and their dangers during pregnancy.[30]

CAUSES AND EFFECTS OF STDs IN PREGNANCY

STD	ORGANISM	RISKS	TREATMENT
Herpes	*Herpes simplex* (HSV-1 or HSV-2) viruses infect the genitals or the mouth (cold sores).	Fetus can be infected in the uterus or at birth. Risks include brain damage, eye infections, skin lesions, encephalitis (inflammation of the brain), infections of the internal organs, and death.	Antiviral drugs, which can control symptoms but cannot cure the disease. A cesarean delivery reduces the risk of infection of the newborn.
Chlamydia (the most common sexually transmitted disease in the United States)	Bacterium *Chlamydia trachomatis*	Premature labor and delivery; eye infections and pneumonia in newborn.	Antibiotic treatments are effective, but immunity does not develop, so reinfection is possible. Antibiotic drops in infant's eyes (required by state law) prevent infection and blindness.
Trichomoniasis	Single-cell protozoan *Trichomonas vaginalis*	Possibly low birth weight and premature delivery.	Treatment with antibiotics is considered safe and effective after the first trimester.
Syphilis	Spiral-shaped bacterium *Treponema pallidum*	The organism passes through the placenta to the fetus. Nearly half of all infants infected with syphilis die during pregnancy or at birth.	The antibiotic penicillin (or a different antibiotic in those who are allergic to penicillin).
Gonorrhea ("the clap")	Bacterium *Neisseria gonorrhea*	Can infect infant's eyes during vaginal birth.	Antibiotic drops in infant's eyes (required by state law) prevent eye damage or blindness.
AIDS	HIV (human immunodeficiency virus)	Can be transmitted to the infant during pregnancy or delivery.	Taking the antiviral drug AZT during pregnancy reduces the risk of infecting the infant.

Preterm, or premature, birth is delivery after 20 weeks of pregnancy but before the end of 37 weeks. Preterm birth carries with it increased risks for breathing problems, low birth weight, bleeding inside the skull, cerebral palsy, blindness, and death. About 1 of every 10 babies born in the United States is preterm. Pregnancy at age 15 or younger increases the risk by 50 percent.[31]

"It's nearly impossible with the technology we have today to accurately predict who is going to give birth to a premature baby," says Nancy S. Green of the March of Dimes Birth Defects Foundation.[32]

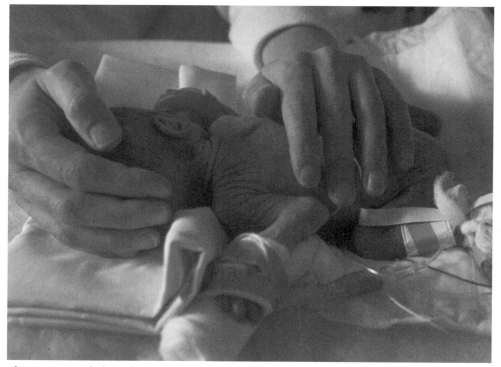

This premature baby is being cared for in the intensive care unit of a hospital.

What Is Low Birth Weight, and Why Is It a Problem?

A newborn that weighs less than 2,500 grams (5 lb. 8 oz.) is considered "low birth weight." One that weighs less than 1,500 grams (3 lb. 4 oz.) is classed as extremely low birth weight. These tiny infants face breathing difficulties, because their lungs are not fully developed. Heart, liver, and other vital organs may not function normally either. Low birth weight infants have trouble regulating body temperature and sugar levels in the blood. They face a greater risk of infections and bleeding in the brain. They may not feed well.

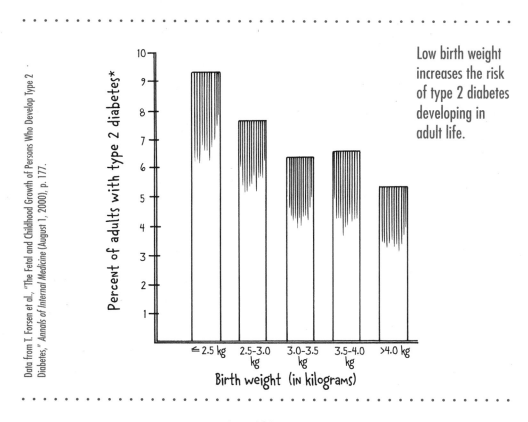

Low birth weight increases the risk of type 2 diabetes developing in adult life.

Data from T. Forsen et al., "The Fetal and Childhood Growth of Persons Who Develop Type 2 Diabetes," *Annals of Internal Medicine* (August 1, 2000), p. 177.

Drugs called surfactants are used today in the treatment of extremely low birth weight infants in intensive care nurseries. The drugs ease breathing, and steroid drugs combat brain hemorrhages. These drugs save lives, but long-term disabilities—such as mental retardation, cerebral palsy, blindness, and deafness—are often unavoidable. So is infant death. Low birth weight and prematurity account for 16 percent of infant deaths in the United States.[33]

For those that survive, the effects of low birth weight persist past infancy. Researchers in Spain found that low birth weight children were more likely to develop diabetes than were their normal birth weight peers.[34] Low birth weight was also associated with high blood pressure, perhaps because of abnormalities in kidney function or the structure of arteries.[35] British scientists looked at the educational achievement among children ages 7, 11, and 16. Although the environment after birth made a big difference in how well the students performed, those born small were at a disadvantage, even into young adult life.[36]

The best way to treat low birth weight is to stop it from happening. "The most effective prenatal treatment for preventing low birth weight is for the mother to avoid nicotine and alcohol and to maintain good, balanced nutrition," says pediatrician Empar Lurbe.[37] Good medical care during pregnancy is also a must.

How Much Time Between Pregnancies Is Best?

In countries where mothers are generally well nourished and well cared for, conceiving a second child between 18 and 23 months after the birth of the first is best, say researchers at the Centers for Disease Control and

Prevention in Atlanta. Babies conceived too soon, within six months after the first, face a 40 percent greater risk of premature birth or low birth weight. On the other hand, waiting 10 years increases risks that much or more. The researchers think that the mother's body becomes primed by the earlier pregnancy, with increased blood flow to an enlarged uterus. These benefits disappear over time.[38]

In developing countries where nutrition and prenatal care are poor, an interval of three to five years between births is best, say experts at Johns Hopkins University. Chances for survival of both mother and child increase greatly. One reason may be that the mother has time to restore the nutritional reserves she needs to make breast milk. Another reason may be that children don't compete for food and care.[39]

Genetics: A Primer for (Potential) Parents

· · · · ·

In the beginning, you have your genes. In the end, it's what you did with them that makes the difference.

AUBREY MILUNSKY

· · · · ·

His parents named him Robert, but everyone calls him Bobby. He's as keen on baseball and as sour on girls as any other nine-year-old boy in his school. He likes science, hates spelling, and collects Spider-Man comics. Bobby wants to be a reporter when he grows up. If he grows up.

What makes Bobby's future uncertain is a disease called cystic fibrosis, or CF. CF springs from a fault in a gene that regulates the body's salt transport machinery. The result is a thick, sticky mucus that clogs airways and prevents digestive enzymes made in the pancreas from reaching the intestines. The symptoms of CF include coughing, wheezing, poor weight gain, excessive appetite, and bulky, foul-smelling stools.

CF isn't catching. It's inherited. From his two healthy parents, Bobby got the genes for CF. Since 1989, scientists have known which gene causes the disease. It is an abnormal piece of DNA in chromosome pair #7. Neither of Bobby's parents ever heard of CF before Bobby was born. It had never before appeared in either of their families. However, the gene is fairly common. About 1 in every 31 Americans (1 in 28 Caucasians) carries it.[40] But carrying the gene is not the same as having the disease. It takes two CF genes, one from each parent, to make a child sick with CF. Because two genes are required, CF is called a recessive disorder.

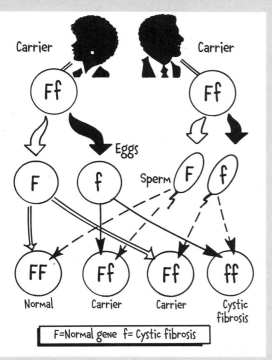

F=Normal gene f= Cystic fibrosis

Another recessive disorder is sickle-cell anemia. It follows the same pattern of inheritance as CF. One in every 12 African Americans carries the gene.[41] The gene causes the body to make abnormal hemoglobin, the protein in red blood cells that carries oxygen.[42] When oxygen levels get low—as, for example, during exercise—the round red cells of people with sickle-cell anemia twist into a crescent shape. The misshapen cells tangle together. They can jam the tiny blood vessels that supply oxygen to body tissues, causing the death of cells. If jams occur in the heart or brain, the person may die.

Not all inherited diseases are recessive. Sex-linked disorders involve the chromosomes that determine gender. Most females have two X chromosomes for their 23rd pair. Most males have an X and a Y. The Y chromosome causes an embryo to develop as a male, but it carries few other genes. The X chromosome carries many more. They have no matched gene on the Y chromosome. So, for characteristics controlled by genes on the X chromosome, females get two copies, but males get only one.

Therefore, an abnormal gene carried on the X chromosome will show its effects only in males. (For females, the chance of getting the abnormal gene on both X chromosomes is small. One normal gene is usually enough to keep things working as they should.) One example is the crippling disease Duchenne muscular dystrophy. Boys with this disease cannot produce a substance that protects muscle cells from damage during contraction. Without this substance, muscles wither. Boys with this disorder usually start having trouble walking between ages 2 and 6. They are often confined to a wheelchair by age 11. The wasting that begins in the limbs eventually affects all the voluntary muscles. Death usually occurs by the late twenties when breathing fails.

Some other genetic diseases are caused by a single gene from either parent. They are called dominant disorders. One example is Marfan syndrome. About 1 person in 10,000 in the United States has it.[43] (Although numbers like this may make genetic disorders seem extremely rare, they aren't. Scientists believe that every one of us is born with about six possibly harmful genes.[44]) People with Marfan syndrome are very tall and have long fingers. They are usually nearsighted and often have a life-threatening weakness of the aorta. The symptoms of Marfan syndrome arise from a defect in connective tissue, the support structure that holds the body together. Connective tissue forms the walls of blood vessels and the tendons that attach muscles to bones.

Another class of disorders arises not from single genes, but from extra or missing pieces of chromosomes, or

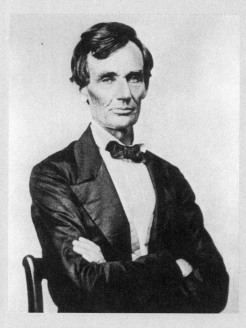

President Abraham Lincoln had Marfan syndrome, as evidenced by his long fingers, shrunken chest, and thin head.

even whole chromosomes. Normally, chromosomes occur in pairs, one from each parent. An extra chromosome nearly always causes a birth defect. Defects in chromosomes show up in about 1 in every 156 live births.[45] One example is the extra chromosome 21, or an extra piece of it, that causes Down syndrome. This common birth defect (about 1 in 800 births) is the most frequently identified cause of mental retardation. Although many people with Down syndrome suffer from heart defects, thyroid disease, and blood diseases, many survive. In the United States between 1983 and 1997, the median life expectancy for people with Down syndrome increased from 25 to 49 years.[46]

Scientists and doctors are trying to develop new and better ways to treat inherited disorders. Most states, for example, now routinely test newborns for sickle-cell anemia shortly after birth. The test separates hemoglobin in the same small blood sample taken for other tests. Better treatments and drugs improve the outlook for people with sickle-cell. In 1973, half of all patients died by the age of 14. Today, antibiotics and other drugs help half survive into their forties.[47] While risky and not always possible, transplants of bone marrow (where red blood cells form) have cured some severely affected children.

Early diagnosis and prevention are important. Tests including chorionic villus sampling and amniocentesis (see page 135) can detect many birth defects and inherited disorders in a fetus. When they are found, many couples choose to end a pregnancy. Even earlier, before pregnancy, people can be tested to see if they carry a gene for some of the 5,000 genetic diseases that are known.[48] People who know they are carriers should seek genetic counseling. Other reasons to seek such help include a family history of inherited disease, a pregnancy past age 35 (when the risk of chromosomal abnormalities begins to increase sharply), or an abnormal blood test result—for example, when a high level of alpha-fetoprotein suggests a chance of spina bifida.

Genetic counselors help their

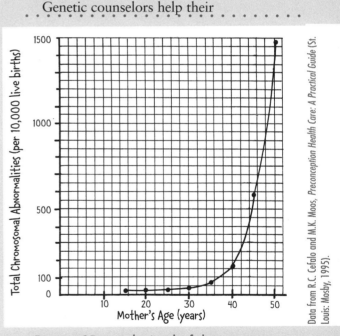

Past age 35, a mother's risk of chromosome problems in her baby increases.

Data from R.C. Cefalo and M.K. Moos, *Preconception Health Care: A Practical Guide* (St. Louis: Mosby, 1995).

clients understand the inheritance, treatment, and outlook for a child with an inherited disease. They predict the chance of a particular birth defect occurring in a family. They help couples understand their options and reach the decision that is right for them. Like all medical professionals, genetic counselors promise confidentiality. Information about their clients is strictly private.

That's of no concern to Bobby right now, but his sister Lisa cares.

She's in high school. She plans to marry and have a family someday. She knows from a genetic test that she carries the gene for CF. She wants to decide when and how she will tell her future husband about her carrier status. She'll ask him to be tested. Chances are, he won't be a carrier. But if he is, they'll plan their family together with the help of a genetic counselor.

CHAPTER FIVE

16 QUESTIONS

ABOUT REPRODUCTION, TECHNOLOGY, AND THE FUTURE

. . . the endless Future touches me too in the unseen Babe . . .
• JULIA WARD HOWE •

What Does Technology Have to Do With Reproduction?

Fundamentally, nothing. Reproduction is a natural process. It requires no chemical, mechanical, or engineered assistance. But knowledge used to achieve a purpose is technology, and our new knowledge about human reproduction is being applied in many ways. From becoming pregnant to delivering healthy babies, human reproduction relies more each year on medical devices, procedures, or interventions—in a word, technology.

Technology is used to achieve several goals. "Assisted reproductive technology," or ART, brings egg and sperm together. The most commonly used procedures are IVF (in vitro fertilization) and ICSI (intracytoplasmic sperm injection). Since 1981, nearly 150,000 babies have been born in the U.S. with the aid of ART. More than 35,000 of them were delivered in 2000 alone.[1]

Ultrasound, amniocentesis, and chorionic villus sampling diagnose defects in a fetus. Tests and electronic equipment monitor the health of both mother and fetus during labor. More experimental, and more controversial, is research into the use of stem cells from embryos and fetuses as treatments for disease. Also making headlines is work on cloning, the production of cells or whole organisms—not from sperm and egg, but from a single, adult body cell.

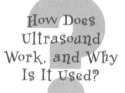
How Does Ultrasound Work, and Why Is It Used?

Ultrasound equipment produces a sonogram, or a picture of organs inside the body. The technique uses sound waves of such high frequency that they cannot be heard. (Frequency is the number of sound wave cycles per second. The highest frequency humans can hear is 20 thousand Hertz. The sound waves used for ultrasound exams have a frequency of 1 to 7 million Hertz.) The amount of energy they contain is low.

The sound waves are made in a device called a transducer. There are two types of transducers: the hand-held kind, which is moved across the skin; or the vaginal probe, which is inserted into the vagina to get a detailed picture of the uterus. Both work the same way. They contain one or more quartz crystals that vibrate in response to an electrical current. This vibration changes electrical energy into the mechanical energy of sound.

When sound waves from the transducer enter the body, they travel through different materials at different speeds. When they hit a

VELOCITY OF SOUND WAVES IN VARIOUS MATERIALS [2]

MATERIAL	VELOCITY (meters per second)
Air	331
Fat	1450
Water (122°F)	1540
Human soft tissue	1540
Brain	1541
Liver	1549
Kidney	1561
Blood	1570
Muscle	1585
Lens of eye	1620
Skull bone	4080
Brass	4490
Aluminum	6400

boundary between one kind of tissue and another—such as bone and muscle, or fluid and membrane—some bounce back, like an echo. The transducer receives those that bounce back, and the crystals work in reverse. They convert the mechanical energy of sound into an electrical current. A computer translates the electrical signals into a picture on a monitor. The picture is called a sonogram.

Ultrasound exams yield several different kinds of information. Still pictures show individual structures of the uterus and the fetus inside it. The pictures can be saved, enlarged, or printed just like any other

The ultrasound has become a standard tool for evaluating the fetus.

photograph. Or, they can be viewed in rapid sequence, showing movement. Most ultrasound scanners create two-dimensional pictures. A newer method of processing, which is growing in popularity, provides three-dimensional views.

Another type of sonogram is the Doppler. It works because sound waves bounce back to the transducer at a slightly different frequency than they had when they left it. The frequency shift can be used to produce colored images of problems such as clots in blood vessels or weaknesses in artery walls. Doppler techniques provide data on heart rate and blood flow.

Sonograms tell doctors a lot about what's going on during a pregnancy. A sonogram reveals the age of the fetus, its rate of growth, the placement of the placenta within the uterus, the amount of fluid in the amniotic sac, and the number of fetuses. It can spot some birth defects, and it shows the sex of the fetus. During labor and delivery, a fetal monitor uses sound waves to provide valuable information about fetal position, oxygen supply, and heart rate.

Is Ultrasound Safe?

Ultrasound has been used since the 1950s. During that time, it has proved safe. Sound is not radiation. Ultrasound scanners do not use X-rays. For that reason, scientists believe there is little chance that ultrasound could cause genetic changes in eggs in the ovaries or birth defects in a fetus. It produces no heat that can harm the fetus, and despite all the gossip, the sound waves cannot hurt the ears of the fetus. "Ultrasound is a safe, painless, and effective way of determining what's going on with the unborn baby," says Roger Harms, an obstetrician at the Mayo Clinic.[3]

What Is Fetal Monitoring, and Why Is It Done?

Fetal monitoring means keeping track of vital health information during pregnancy and delivery. How fetal monitoring is done—and how often—depends on a woman's health history, the stage of her pregnancy, and the results of routine tests. Women who have kidney or heart disease, diabetes, high blood pressure, or who carry a fetus two weeks past their due date may benefit from extra-vigilant fetal monitoring. Fetal monitoring may be especially important when ultrasound exams reveal twins or triplets, too much or too little amniotic fluid, or slow fetal growth.

Ultrasound exams are one form of fetal monitoring. Other monitoring tests include:

- **Kick count.** In late pregnancy, a woman records how often her fetus moves. Frequent movements are a sign of fetal well-being.
- **Nonstress test.** A belt is placed around the woman's abdomen, while electronic equipment monitors the fetal heart rate continuously for 20 minutes or more. Normally, the heart beats faster when the fetus moves. If it doesn't, further tests of fetal health may be needed.
- **Biophysical profile.** This test combines an ultrasound scan with a nonstress test. It measures the amount of amniotic fluid, along with fetal heart rate, breathing, body movement, and muscle tone.
- **Contraction stress test.** This test measures how the fetal heart rate changes when the uterus contracts. Contractions are induced during the test to simulate labor. A normal result shows that the fetus is getting enough oxygen. An abnormal result signals the need for further testing.

During labor and delivery, additional monitoring may be wise. Health professionals measure the rates of uterine contractions and fetal heart beat. The simplest method is external electronic monitoring. Medical personnel routinely use a stethoscope or handheld ultrasound transducer to measure the fetal heart rate every 15 minutes or so. The fetal heart should beat about 140 times a minute. It should not change much during or after contractions. Rates slower than 120 or greater than 160 may signal distress.

In some cases, doctors recommend internal electronic monitoring. For this procedure, the sac of amniotic fluid is broken, and a small electrode is attached to the scalp of the fetus. While this procedure provides the most complete and reliable information, it keeps the mother immobile and may increase the risk of infection. False signs of fetal distress lead, some say, to unnecessary cesarean deliveries. Yet few doctors doubt that this type of monitoring saves the lives of thousands of infants annually.

What Is Amniocentesis, and Why Is It Done?

Amniocentesis is a procedure used to test the fetus for certain birth defects. Between 16 and 18 weeks of pregnancy, a health professional inserts a needle through the walls of the abdomen and uterus to withdraw a small amount of amniotic fluid from the sac that surrounds the fetus. The fluid in the sac replaces itself within a few days.

Testing is done in two ways. First, the fluid itself is tested. One test measures the amount of alpha-fetoprotein (AFP) in the fluid. The fetus makes AFP. Too much may indicate spina bifida. Too little may be a sign of Down syndrome. The second method is genetic testing of fetal cells. In the normal course of growth, the fetus sheds some cells into the fluid. These cells can be collected, grown in the laboratory, and examined with a microscope. Defects of chromosomes, such as Down syndrome, may be found this way. Recessive gene disorders, such as cystic fibrosis or sickle-cell anemia, can be diagnosed from fetal cells, too.

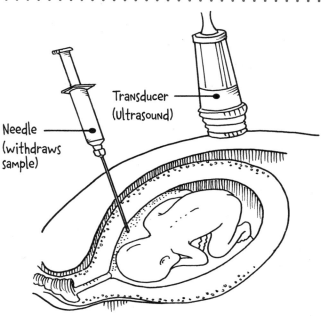

A sample of amniotic fluid is drawn for testing.

Needle (withdraws sample)

Transducer (Ultrasound)

Doctors recommend amniocentesis for couples who face an increased risk of inherited disorders or birth defects in their offspring. They include:

- women who will be 35 or older on their due date (because the risk of chromosomal defects increases with age).
- couples who already have had a child with a birth defect or have a family history of certain birth defects.
- known carriers of a genetic disorder.

In most cases, the test comes back normal, and parents are relieved. The results, however, do not indicate that the fetus is free of all defects, only of those that were tested for. Also, no test is perfect, so false positives (saying the defect is present when it's not) and false negatives (saying the defect is not present when it is) do occur. For these and other reasons, couples must be clear in their own minds about how they will handle test results. If a serious birth defect is diagnosed, the majority of couples choose abortion. A significant minority, however, do not. Instead, they use the advance warning to help them prepare to care for their handicapped child.

What Is Chorionic Villus Sampling, and Why Is It Done?

Chorionic villus sampling (CVS) is similar to amniocentesis. It diagnoses birth defects and inherited diseases in a fetus. It is done earlier than amniocentesis, between weeks 10 and 12. The test sample is not amniotic fluid, but cells from the chorionic villi. These are the fingerlike projections of the placenta from the fetus into the uterine wall. Because villi form from the fertilized egg, these cells have the same genetic makeup as the fetus.

The cell sample may be taken through the vagina or through the abdominal wall, using ultrasound images as a guide. The cells are sent to the lab and grown, just as they are for amniocentesis. Examination of the cells reveals chromosomal defects and some inherited diseases. CVS cannot diagnose neural tube defects, since no amniotic fluid is used.

What Are the Risks of Amniocentesis and CVS?

Amniocentesis is safe, but not without risks. It may cause cramping, bleeding, infection, or leakage of the amniotic fluid. Injury to the fetus is rare. The procedure carries a slight risk of miscarriage. When performed by a skilled physician in a community hospital, the risk of pregnancy loss for healthy women is about 3 in 1,000.[4]

The risk of miscarriage is slightly higher with CVS, as is the chance of infection. However, CVS is preferred in some cases, because results can be obtained earlier in pregnancy. Unwanted abortions can be avoided when at-risk fetuses are found to be disease-free early in their development. When a serious defect is found, an earlier abortion is safer for those women who choose to have one.

What Is Infertility?

Couples who have sex for a year without contraception and do not achieve pregnancy are defined as infertile. So too are couples who conceive but, because of repeated miscarriages, have not been able to have a child. About 15 percent of the 60 million couples of reproductive age in the United States seek medical assistance for infertility at one time or another.[5] The cause comes from male and female equally—each about one third of the time. In the remaining third, the causes are either unknown or combined between both partners.[6]

In finding the cause, it's important to rule out the obvious first. Is the couple having intercourse frequently enough and at the right times? Sometimes, simply pinpointing the time of ovulation solves the problem. If it persists, however, further tests may be needed.

Irregular or abnormal ovulation is one common cause of infertility. One way to find out whether a woman is actually ovulating is to measure hormone levels in her blood. The level of LH should peak around the time of ovulation. If it doesn't, it's possible that no egg has been released. After ovulation, the ovaries produce the hormone progesterone. Its level measured toward the end of the menstrual cycle reveals whether ovulation actually occurred.

More often, ovulation is occurring, but fertilization or implantation is not. A blocked, constricted, or fluid-filled fallopian tube may be at fault. A procedure called a hysterosalpingogram can locate such problems. A liquid containing iodine is injected into the reproductive tract. It provides the contrast needed for clear X-ray images. The pictures locate obstructions in the tubes. They also reveal growths, scarring, or abnormalities in the size and shape of the uterus.

In still other cases, the female system is working, but the male is not ejaculating sufficient numbers of healthy sperm. A sperm sample is considered normal if 30 percent or more are normally shaped, more than half move forward, and at least 40 million sperm are present in each ejaculate.[7] In some cases, the man's sperm or the woman's body contains proteins that cause the sperm to clump together. They stop swimming or cannot penetrate the egg.

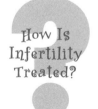

How Is Infertility Treated?

One solution to infertility is to wait and see. In fact, some experts think the one-year definition of infertility is too short. Two years is better. Unless a cause of infertility is known, couples should be patient, says David Dunson, a researcher at the National Institute of Environmental Health Sciences.[8]

If waiting doesn't work, a couple who want to have a child can seek treatment for infertility. Most cases can be treated with traditional medical therapies such as drugs or surgery. In the male, for example, medications can overcome hormone deficiencies, antisperm antibodies, or infection. Surgery may open a blocked vas deferens. If difficulties with ejaculation are involved, medical personnel may place the man's sperm in the woman's vagina. The technique is called artificial insemination.

For a few cases, assisted reproductive technology, or ART, may be the answer. Options include:

- **In vitro fertilization (IVF).** The egg is fertilized outside the female body and early embryos develop. Then two or more embryos are placed into the uterus in hopes of achieving implantation.
- **Gamete intrafallopian transfer (GIFT).** Sperm from the man and eggs that have been surgically removed from the woman's ovary are inserted into a fallopian tube together, in hopes that fertilization and implantation will follow.
- **Zygote intrafallopian transfer (ZIFT).** Sperm and egg are mixed together outside the body. Fertilization is confirmed before a zygote is surgically placed in a fallopian tube.
- **Intracytoplasmic sperm injection (ICSI).** A sperm cell is injected into an egg. The resulting embryo is placed into the uterus as in IVF.

While these procedures involve certain increased risks—including multiple fetuses, pregnancy complications, low birth weight, and birth defects—many infertile couples are eager to try them, in hopes of having a much-wanted child.

How Is In Vitro Fertilization (IVF) Done?

In vitro is Latin. It means "in glass," as contrasted with *in vivo*, meaning "in life." In vitro fertilization, IVF, is the union of sperm and egg achieved not in a fallopian tube, but in a laboratory dish. To accomplish this, doctors first prescribe hormonal drugs that stimulate the ovaries to release more than one egg. The next step is egg retrieval. Using ultrasound images to guide a probe, doctors remove eggs from the ovaries. They place them in a laboratory dish where sperm wait. Fertilization occurs naturally, but outside the body.

The resulting embryos are checked for abnormalities. Then two or more healthy ones are introduced into the woman's uterus, bypassing the fallopian tubes. Any remaining healthy embryos can be frozen for future use. That way, if pregnancy doesn't happen on the first try, implantation can be attempted again later, without the need for another cycle of egg retrieval.

GIFT is basically the same as IVF, except eggs and sperm are put into the fallopian tubes surgically and fertilization occurs in vivo. ZIFT is much the same, too, except introduction into the woman's reproductive system occurs at an earlier stage—a fertilized egg, not an embryo.

Can Genetic Disorders Be Diagnosed in an Embryo?

An adjunct to IVF is being offered in some medical centers, and couples at risk for genetic disease are taking advantage of it. The technique is preimplantation genetic diagnosis (PGD). The IVF procedure is the same, but embryos are tested for their genetic makeup, and only healthy ones are placed in the uterus. More than 200 inherited disorders can be detected at the embryo stage.[9]

In 2002 the power of PGD was proven. Illinois doctors analyzed IVF embryos from a woman who carried a gene associated with early Alzheimer's disease. They selected four embryos free of the gene for implantation in her uterus, and she subsequently bore a healthy child without the abnormal gene.[10]

PGD is controversial. Some people fear it could be used for frivolous or unethical reasons, such as choosing a child's sex. Say University of California physicians Dena Towner and Roberta Loewy, "Ultimately, patients and physicians are faced with the 'technology question(s)': should a procedure be done simply because it can be done and . . . who is to decide, and when?"[11]

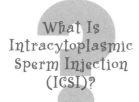

What Is Intracytoplasmic Sperm Injection (ICSI)?

ICSI is a variant of IVF. It is used when sperm cannot penetrate the egg. Using powerful microscopes, lab workers perform microsurgery. Holding the egg with a pipette, they pull a sperm cell into the tip of a tiny glass tube. The tube then acts as a needle, pushing the sperm through the membrane of the egg. If all goes well, fertilization occurs. The resulting embryo can then be placed in the uterus as with IVF.

What Are the Risks of IVF and ICSI?

Low birth weight is a risk. It happens both because of the procedures and because multiple fetuses (each weighing less than a single fetus) are more likely.[12] Drugs that induce multiple ovulation may increase a woman's risk of developing cancer of the ovary, although some evidence disputes that claim.[13] Women may also experience side effects from hormonal treatments, such as hot flashes and

THE ICSI PROCESS

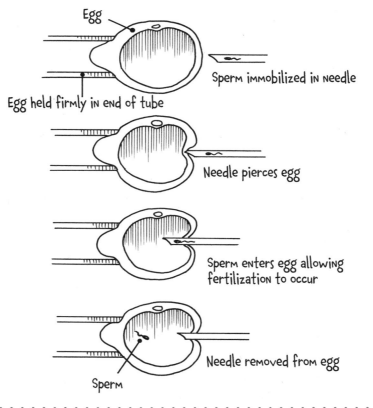

Egg

Sperm immobilized in needle

Egg held firmly in end of tube

Needle pierces egg

Sperm enters egg allowing fertilization to occur

Needle removed from egg

Sperm

changes in vision.[14] Both IVF and ICSI carry with them a slightly increased risk of chromosomal defects.[15] IVF and ICSI do not appear to increase the overall risk of birth defects,[16] although specific defects, such as vision problems, have been uncovered in some studies.[17] While some experts say the chance of miscarriage increases, others refute that claim.[18] One criticism of ICSI is that, if there's a genetic reason for the sperm's inability to penetrate the egg, that defect might be passed on to a male fetus.

In the early embryo, all cells are the same. They have all the genes they need to develop as skin, nerve, muscle, or any other kind of cell. But as development progresses, cells begin to specialize, or differentiate. Some of the genes "turn off" and others "turn on." Differentiated cells begin to look and function differently. Also, they lose their ability to become some other kind of cell.

Stem cells are undifferentiated cells. They have the ability to develop into various types of specialized cells. The cells of the early embryo are all stem cells, but not all stem cells are lost during development. Some persist in the fetus. They can be isolated from the blood that remains in the umbilical cord after birth. Stem cells are present in children and adults as well. They can be found in bone marrow, fat, hair, skin, teeth, the pancreas, and the heart.

Scientists are eager to experiment with stem cells for at least three purposes:

1. **To learn more about how cells change during development.** Genes are "switched on" and "switched off" during differentiation. How does this happen and why? The answers might help treat disease such as cancer, where genes that should be "off" are "on," causing uncontrolled cell division.

2. **To develop and test new drugs more efficiently.** Drugs that proved ineffective or unsafe when tested in cell cultures would not go on to testing in animals.

3. **To produce therapeutic tissues and organs to treat disease.** The possibilities are many: nerve cells to heal spinal cord injuries; pancreatic cells to make insulin in diabetics; muscle cells to repair damaged hearts; and more.

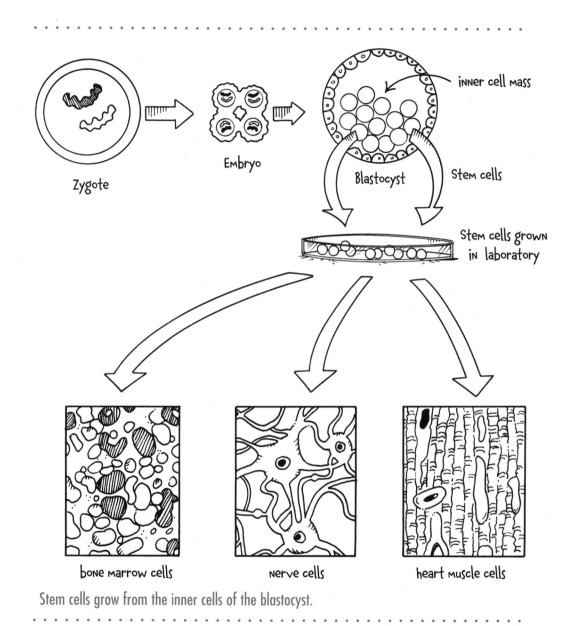

inner cell mass

Zygote

Embryo

Blastocyst

Stem cells

Stem cells grown in laboratory

bone marrow cells

nerve cells

heart muscle cells

Stem cells grow from the inner cells of the blastocyst.

Progress has been made in all three areas. For example, researchers at the National Institute of Neurological Disorders and Stroke derived neural stem cells from embryonic cells, and then induced them to differentiate. The neurons that resulted behaved electrically and chemically in the same way that normal midbrain nerve cells would.[19] The researchers think their work might lead to a treatment for Parkinson's disease.

The controversy about stem cell research arises from ethical objections about the source of the stem cells. Some people feel that it's wrong to work on cells from aborted fetuses or from embryos created in fertility clinics. Using stem cells from adults gets around these objections, but technical problems arise. Adult stem cells are harder to isolate and grow. They don't divide indefinitely as do embryonic stem cells. They may not be able to differentiate in as many different ways as embryonic stem cells. "It might take us quite a while to figure out how to work with adult [stem] cells," says NIH researcher Ron McKay.[20]

Nevertheless, research on adult stem cells shows great promise. In 2001, scientists at Yale and Johns Hopkins used stem cells from bone marrow in mice to create liver, lung, intestinal, and skin cells.[21] In 2002, a team at the University of Minnesota found stem cells in bone marrow that have all the differentiating abilities of embryonic cells. The cells appear, also, to grow indefinitely in culture.[22] That same year, a Mayo Clinic team found adult stem cells in blood that can be induced to form smooth muscle cells.[23] Because such cells are the building blocks of arteries, they might be used to construct new blood vessels in damaged hearts.

As laboratory work continues, physicians are taking stem cell research into clinical settings. They have experimented with stem cell treatments for medical problems ranging from sickle-cell disease[24] to bone fractures.[25] While early trials look promising, stem cell research has a long way to go—both in the laboratory and in the doctor's office.

The blood that remains in the umbilical cord after birth contains some of the same stem cells as bone marrow. These cells can differentiate into red blood cells, which carry oxygen; white blood cells, which fight disease; or platelets, which help blood to clot. The cells can be isolated from cord blood and banked, or frozen for future use. They can be used in much the same way as bone marrow transplants: to treat certain cancers, blood diseases, and immune disorders. In fact, cord blood cells have an advantage over bone marrow. Their tissue type need not be a perfect match to the recipient. Because cord cells are less likely to be attacked by the recipient's immune system, rejection of a transplant occurs infrequently.

The American Academy of Pediatrics does not recommend banking cord blood for a family's private use, unless a disease such as leukemia is known. They favor, however, donation to public banks, where the stem cells may be made available to all who need them.[26] In the 1990s, some 1,000 cord blood transplants were performed to treat 30 different diseases.[27] Cord blood stem cells could find even wider use in the future in treatments for multiple sclerosis, arthritis, diabetes, or Alzheimer's disease.

The terms "clone" and "cloning" are used in two different ways. Much of the controversy arises from confusion between the two. Both begin with the genetic information from a body cell (not a sperm or egg) from a single individual. *Reproductive* cloning produces a complete, new individual. *Therapeutic* cloning produces new cells, such as stem cells, for research or treatment of disease.

In either case, the first step is the formation of a clonal zygote. The process is called somatic cell nuclear transfer (SCNT). Here's how it works. First, the nucleus is removed from a donated egg cell. Then a nucleus is removed from a body cell of another individual and inserted into the egg. The result is a clonal zygote.

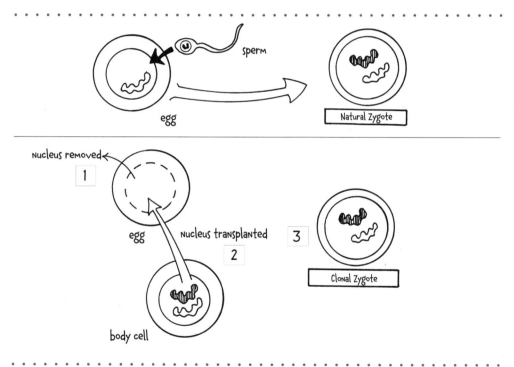

Somatic cell nuclear transfer forms a clonal zygote (bottom panel). First, the nucleus is removed from a donated egg cell (1). Then a nucleus is removed from a body cell of another individual and inserted into the egg (2). The result is a clonal zygote (3).

Look back at the diagram of stem cell production on page 145. If the zygote used as the starting point is a clonal zygote, then the process is *therapeutic* cloning. But if the clonal zygote is implanted in a uterus and allowed to develop into a whole organism, the result is a *reproductive* clone.

Most people see nothing wrong with therapeutic cloning for humans. Researchers say cloning cells from people with inherited diseases would help them invent new treatments. They say stem cells from clonal zygotes might be used to form tissues or organs for transplant that the body would not reject. "Because of SCNT, science could advance to a point where millions of people will have access to life-saving therapies developed using their own DNA," says the American Society for Reproductive Medicine.[28] In a 2002 poll, two thirds of Americans said they favor therapeutic cloning for research and treatment of disease.[29]

Reproductive cloning is a different matter. While the cloning of plants and farm animals draws few objections, citizens and governments worldwide loudly oppose human reproductive cloning. In a survey sponsored by the American Museum of Natural History, 92 percent of Americans say they are against it.[30] Says the Federation of American Societies for Experimental Biology, "As a community of scientists, we strongly oppose human reproductive cloning and view this as an irresponsible and misguided act."[31]

The Unborn Patient

. . . . .

Any sufficiently advanced technology is indistinguishable from Magic.
ARTHUR C. CLARKE

. . . . .

Visit a large hospital in any major city and you'll find it: the intensive care unit for newborns. It's where those newest to life struggle to keep it. Some don't survive, but each year more and more do. Theirs is a story that goes back not generations, but only a few decades. As knowledge has expanded and technologies have multiplied, newborns who might once have lost their grip on life now seize it and hold on.

The achievements of newborn medicine and intensive care are admirable, but are they—in too many cases—too little too late? Pioneers on the frontiers of medicine are now working to develop medical treatments for the unborn. It sounds like science fiction, but increasingly, it is not. Today, doctors are experimenting with ways to treat the fetus. Tomorrow, disease and disability may be cured before birth—through surgery, stem cell transplants, or gene therapy.

Fetal medicine began in 1963, when New Zealand physician A. William Liley treated a fetus with Rh disease. The fetus would not have survived early delivery, so Liley inserted a needle through the walls of the mother's abdomen and uterus and gave the fetus a blood transfusion. The transfusion was a success.

Since Liley's time, approaches to the fetus as patient have multiplied. One much-publicized effort is fetal

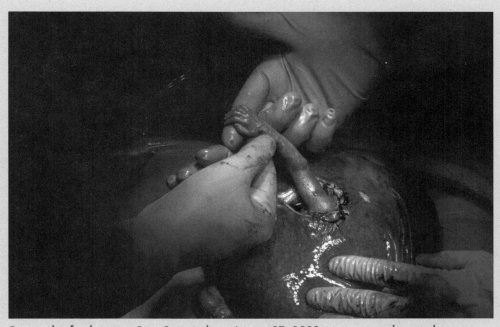

During this fetal surgey, Sara Switzer, born August 27, 1999, was operated on at the Vanderbilt University Medical Center. The third hand holding the baby belongs to Sara's father, Mike Spitzer.

surgery. Doctors open the uterus, operate on the fetus, close the uterus, and allow the pregnancy to continue. It sounds simple, but it's not. Risks to the mother are real, and the surgery is extremely delicate. Nevertheless, it has been successfully performed in dozens of cases, especially for neural tube defects. Surgeons can close the gap in the spine of the fetus before birth much as they would after. One advantage, they hope, is that paralysis and brain damage, which results from accumulation of fluid in the skull before birth, can be prevented.

In 2001, Mark Johnson and his team at Children's Hospital in Philadelphia reported on surgical repairs of spina bifida in 39 fetuses operated on between 20 and 25 weeks. Three were lost in premature labor. Among the other 36, two thirds had better movement in their legs than would have been expected.[32] While these surgeons make no claims for miracle cures, their work shows that fetal surgery can be performed with some success. Whether prebirth surgery is more effective than treatment after birth remains to be seen.

Another candidate for surgery is a fetus with a cyst growing in its lung. The lung can grow so large that it restricts blood flow to the heart. In such cases, fluid accumulates in the chest cavity and the fetus dies. Surgeons have experimented with removing excess lung tissue from the fetus between weeks 21 and 29 of pregnancy. In one study, eight of 13 fetuses that had this operation survived. The fluid buildup in their chests diminished, and their lungs grew normally.[33]

Surgery isn't the only way to treat the unborn. Researchers are looking for ways to use stem cells to treat disease before it starts. One disease of interest is SCID (severe combined immunodeficiency disease). Children with SCID lack a normal immune system. Their bone marrow fails to produce the white blood cells that attack and destroy disease-causing microbes. In 1996, doctors reported a successful stem cell transplant to a fetus with SCID. The father donated bone marrow, and the fetus received three injections into his chest cavity between 16 and 18 weeks of development. Follow-up tests after birth showed that the baby's bone marrow manufactured some blood cells that were his own and some that were his father's. The number of disease-fighting cells in his blood was normal throughout infancy. As he grew, he fought off colds and ear infections just as any other child would.[34] At age three, he continued to do well, his immune system functioning normally.[35]

In that landmark case, the stem cell transplant corrected the symptom of the disease (the absence of immune cells), but not its cause (the defective gene). Doctors hope, someday, to prevent inherited disorders completely. Gene therapy is the introduction of normal genes into cells to replace defective ones. The gene transfer is achieved with the help of a virus. In the laboratory, the virus is stripped of its ability to cause disease, but its capacity to "infect" the nucleus of a cell remains. The desired gene is then attached to the virus. When it infects its host, it delivers

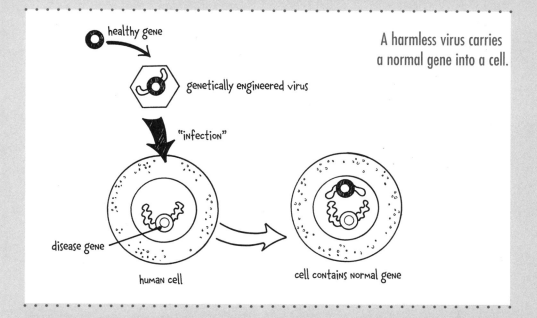

healthy gene

genetically engineered virus

"infection"

disease gene

human cell

A harmless virus carries a normal gene into a cell.

cell contains normal gene

the gene. Every time the infected cell divides, it copies the normal gene. If the introduced gene functions properly—which is no small if!—its products can substitute for those missing or defective in the diseased cell.

Researchers have experimented with ways to use gene therapy in treating cystic fibrosis before birth. In 1997, they used a modified virus to introduce normal genes into the lungs of fetal lambs. Trials with humans will be a long time coming, but doctors believe gene therapy before birth might someday reduce the risk of respiratory infections and pneumonia in infants who inherit cystic fibrosis.[36]

Despite the potential of fetal medicine, optimism is best tempered with realism. Too often, newspapers blaze with headlines lauding "breakthroughs" that fail to deliver on their promise. Experiments are, after all, only experiments. They carry with them the risk of failure. But with experimentation comes the chance of progress. Today, advanced technologies save lives in infant intensive care facilities. Tomorrow, new technologies may save still more new lives, in ways now unimagined and unimaginable.

In Closing

Have you ever gazed up at the stars on a clear, cold night and felt the vastness of the universe around you? If you haven't, you should try it. It's at once a humbling and an uplifting experience. Those stars—their number, age, and distance immeasurable in human terms—remind us how tiny and insignificant we are. At the same time, they open a window to the immeasurable distances within us, in our ability to know, wonder, and comprehend.

Thinking about our own lives has the same effect. Imagine your parents for a moment not as you have known them, but as the sources of the single, tiny cells that made you. Within those cells lay the molecules of life. Their union unleashed the doubling and splitting and doubling again, the building and rebuilding, the shaping and rearranging that—in a mere 266 days—formed you. You, with the capacity to cry and laugh and ponder the stars, arose from your parents, and they from their parents before them, and they from their parents before them. This is the great unbroken stream, the continuity of life. It is as wondrous as the cosmos and as curious.

As you read this book, perhaps you felt more than a little uneasy. So much can go wrong, so many risks loom along the way, that the stream of life seems fragile. Some things mere humans can control and overcome. Many other things we cannot. Nonetheless, every three seconds, a new human breathes its first breath here on planet Earth. The wonder lies not in life imperiled, but in life's boundless persistence and tenacity.

Reproduction is the story of how 1 + 1 = 3 or 4 or more. In that simple and surprising equation lies the essence of who and what we are, as far back as our human origins on the plains of Africa some 150,000 years ago and as far forward in time as our imaginations can take us. If we need reassurance about our place in the cosmos, it lies in those numbers. For within us lies the capacity to project what makes us human into the unknown and unknowable. That's a thought both curious and reassuring.

NOTES

Chapter 1

1. Donald L. Blanchard, "Parthenogenesis in Livebearing Snakes . . . Explained," *The Cold Blooded News* (November 1998).
2. Glenn F. Bastian, *An Illustrated Review of the Reproductive System* (New York: HarperCollins, 1994), p. 4.
3. Ibid.
4. Ibid., p. 14.
5. Ibid.
6. Ibid., p. 10.
7. Ibid.
8. Meredith F. Small, "Sperm Wars," *Discover* (July 1991), 48–53.
9. Ibid.
10. Robin Baker, *Sperm Wars* (New York: Basic Books, 1996).
11. Richard I. Feinbloom, *Pregnancy, Birth, and the Early Months: The Thinking Woman's Guide*, 3rd ed. (Cambridge, MA: Perseus, 2000), p. 65.
12. Regina Avraham, *The Reproductive System* (Philadelphia: Chelsea House, 2001), p. 51.
13. R. Scott and P. Madsen, "What Mother Didn't Tell You About Fertility . . . Because No One Ever Told Her," Pamphlet from the American Fertility Association, 2004, p. 3.
14. Ibid.
15. "Menstrual Periods, Abnormal," *General Health Encyclopedia* at www.healthcentral.com
16. A. B. Namnoum and R. A. Hatcher, "The Menstrual Cycle," *Contraceptive Technology*, 17th ed., (New York: Adams Media, 1998), p. 69.
17. A. J. Wilcox, D. Dunson, and D. D. Baird, "The Timing of the 'Fertile Window' in the Menstrual Cycle: Day Specific Estimates from a Prospective Study," *British Medical Journal* (November 18, 2000), 1259–1262.
18. Richard C. Kuo et al., "NO Is Necessary and Sufficient for Egg Activation at Fertilization," *Nature* (August 10, 2000), 633–636.
19. X. Shi, S. Amindari, K. Paruchuru, D. Skalla, H. Burkin, B. D. Shur, and D. J. Miller, "Cell Surface β-1,4 Galactosyltransferase-I Activates G Protein-Dependent Exocytotic Signaling," The Third International Symposium on The Molecular and Cellular Biology of the Egg and Embryo Extracellular Matrix, Lake Tahoe, CA, September 2000.

20. Victor Grech, Charles Savona-Ventura, and P. Vassallo-Agius, "Unexplained Differences in Sex Ratios in Birth in Europe and North America," *British Medical Journal* (April 27, 2002), 1010–1011.

21. "And Then There Was One," *New Scientist* (October 20, 2001).

22. T. Zach and A. Pramanik, "Multiple Births," updated November 5, 2001, at www.eMedicine.com

23. Joyce A. Martin et al., "Births: Final Data for 2002," *National Vital Statistics Reports* (December 17, 2004), p. 4.

24. "The Effects of Pregnancy on Ventilation and Oxygen Consumption in the Stumpy Tailed Lizard, *Tiliqua rugosa*." Pre-publication manuscript by Suzanne L. Munns and Christopher B. Daniels, University of Adelaide, Adelaide, Australia.

25. Personal communication, Dr. Suzanne Munns, Department of Ecology and Evolutionary Biology, University of California, Irvine.

26. Gail Brown and Joan Magruder, "Sexual vs. Asexual Reproduction: Scientists Find Sex Wins," University of California at Santa Barbara News Release, October 18, 2001.

27. C. M. Lively and J. Jokela, "Temporal and Spatial Distributions of Parasites and Sex in a Freshwater Snail," *Evolutionary Ecology Research* (2002), 219–226.

28. W. R. Rice and A. K. Chippindale, "Sexual Recombination and the Power of Natural Selection," *Science* (October 19, 2001), 555–559.

29. Brown and Magruder.

30. Quoted in Bernice Wuethrich, "Why Sex? Putting Theory to the Test," *Science* (September 25, 1998), 1982.

Chapter 2

1. Rebecca Lipsitz, "Diagnosis at Home: Pregnancy Tests," *Scientific American* (November 2000), 110–111.

2. A. J. Wilcox, D. D. Baird, D. Dunson, R. McChesney, and C. R. Weinberg, "Natural Limits of Pregnancy Testing in Relation to the Expected Menstrual Period," *Journal of the American Medical Association* (October 10, 2001), 1759.

3. Lipsitz, op. cit.

4. Avraham, p. 13.

5. Sheldon H. Cherry, *Understanding Pregnancy and Childbirth*, rev. ed. (Indianapolis: Bobbs-Merrill, 1983), p. 57.

6. "Researcher Discovers How Embryo Attaches to the Uterus," National Institute of Child Health and Human Development, NIH News Release, January 16, 2003.

7. ACOG Patient Education Pamphlet, "Easing Back Pain During Pregnancy," 1998.

8. W. Y. Wong et al., "Male Factor Subfertility: Possible Causes and the Impact of Nutritional Factors," *Fertility and Sterility* (March 2000), 435–442.

9. W. Y. Wong et al., "Effects of Folic Acid and Zinc Sulfate on Male Factor Subfertility: A Double-Blind, Randomized, Placebo-Controlled Trial," *Fertility and Sterility* (March 2002), 491–498.

10. P. Schuetze and P. S. Zeskind, "Relation Between Maternal Cigarette Smoking During Pregnancy and Behavioral and Physiological Measures of Autonomic Regulation in Neonates," *Infancy* (2001), 371–383.

11. Smoking During Pregnancy—United States,1990–2002, CDC *Morbidity and*

Mortality Weekly Report (October 8, 2004), pp. 911–915.

12. "Fetal Alcohol Syndrome Continues to Be a Major Public Health Concern," Reuters Medical News, May 23, 2002.

13. Lynn T. Singer, Robert Arend, Sonia Minnes, Kathleen Farkas, Ann Salvato, H. Lester Kirchner, and Robert Kliegman, "Cognitive and Motor Outcomes of Cocaine-Exposed Infants," *Journal of the American Medical Association* (April 17, 2002), 1952–1960.

14. K. E. Lasser et al., "Timing of New Black Box Warnings and Withdrawals for Prescription Medications," *Journal of the American Medical Association* (May 1, 2002), 2273–2275.

15. Sheila R. Weiss, "Prescription Medication Use in Pregnancy," *Medscape Pharmacology* 2000 at www.medscape.com

16. American College of Obstetricians and Gynecologists, "Exercise During Pregnancy and the Postpartum Period," *ACOG Technical Bulletin* (volume 189), February 1994.

17. Leah Albers for the CNM Group, 1996, "The Duration of Labor in Healthy Women," *Journal of Perinatology* (March 1999), 114–119.

18. R. K. Freeman, "Where Are We with Controlling Cesarean Birth Rates?" American College of Obstetricians and Gynecologists' Task Force on Cesarean Delivery Rates, *Contemporary OB/GYN* (July 2000).

19. Martin et al., p. 2.

20. "Cesarean Birth," ACOG Patient Education Pamphlet, 1999, American College of Obstetricians and Gynecologists.

21. American College of Nurse Midwives, "Rising Cesarean Rate Is Cause for Alarm," Press release, January 15, 2003.

22. A. S. Coco and S. D. Silverman, "External Cephalic Version," *American Family Physician* (September 1, 1998), 731–743.

23. A. S. Coco and S. D. Silverman, "What Can I Do If My Baby Is Breech? Patient Information Sheet," *American Family Physician* (September 1, 1998), p. 744.

24. Op. cit.

25. K. S. Lee et al., "Is Cesarean Delivery the Preferred Route for the Breech? Analysis of the United States Birth Cohorts, 1989–91," *Obstetrical Gynecology* (November 1998), 769–775.

26. J. Zhang , J. Troendle, and M. Yancey, "Reassessing the Labor Curve," *American Journal of Obstetrics and Gynecology* (December 2001, Part 2), S71.

27. Martin et al., p. 2.

28. S. Dublin et al., "Maternal and Neonatal Outcomes after Induction of Labor without an Identified Indication," *American Journal of Obstetrics and Gynecology* (October 2000), 986–994.

29. Jonathan Schaffir, "Survey of Folk Beliefs About Induction of Labor," *Birth* (March 2002), 47–51.

30. "Labor-Inducing Folklore Alive and Well Among Pregnant Women," Press release from Ohio State University, April 14, 2002.

31. A. Bonni and M. Ross, "Forceps Delivery," December 14, 2001, at www.emedicine.com

32. J. Zhang, M. K. Yancey, and C. E. Henderson, "U.S. National Trends in Labor Induction, 1989–1998," *Journal of Reproductive Medicine* (February 2002), 120–124.

33. Jens Wessel and Ulrich Buscher, "Denial of Pregnancy: Population Based Study," *British Medical Journal* (February 23, 2002), p. 458.

Chapter 3

1. J. A. Rosenfeld and K. Everett, "Teenage Women's Use of Contraceptives in Two Populations," Journal of the *American Board of Family Practice* (January/February 2001), 1–6.
2. M. J. Rosenberg, M. S. Waugh, and S. Long, "Unintended Pregnancies and Use, Misuse, and Discontinuation of Oral Contraceptives," *Journal of Reproductive Medicine* (1995), 355–360.
3. C. S. Haignere, R. Gold, and H. J. McDaniel, "Adolescent Abstinence and Condom Use: Are We Sure We Are Really Teaching What Is Safe?" *Health Education & Behavior* (February 1999), 43–54.
4. "The Pill Revisited," Originally published in Mayo Clinic's Women's HealthSource, updated August 7, 2000. Available at www.mayohealth.org/ mayo/9808/htm/thepill.htm.
5. P. A. Marchbanks et al., "Oral Contraceptives and the Risk of Breast Cancer," *New England Journal of Medicine* (June 27, 2002), 2025–2032.
6. B. C. Tanis et al., "Oral Contraceptives and the Risk of Myocardial Infarction," *New England Journal of Medicine* (December 20, 2001), 1787–1793.
7. B. Sibai et al., "A Comparative Assessment of Ortho Evra/ Evra to Placebo Patch Effects on Body Weight," *Fertility and Sterility* (September 2001), p. 188.
8. M. Warren et al.,"The Effects on Weight of a Low-Dose Oral Contraceptive in the Treatment of Women with Moderate Acne Vulgaris," *Fertility and Sterility* (September 2001), S187.
9. "All About Vasectomy," Brochure, Planned Parenthood Federation of America (updated 2000).
10. Ibid.
11. E. F. Fuchs and R. A. Burt, "Vasectomy Reversal Performed 15 Years or More after Vasectomy: Correlation of Pregnancy Outcome with Partner Age and with Pregnancy Results of in Vitro Fertilization with Intracytoplasmic Sperm Injection, *Fertility and Sterility*, (March 2002), 516–519.
12. "Induced Abortion," ACOG Patient Education Pamphlet, American College of Obstetricians and Gynecologists, 2001.
13. S. K. Henshaw, "Unintended Pregnancy in the United States," *Family Planning Perspectives* (1998), 24–29.
14. L. D. Elam-Evans et al., "Abortion Surveillance—United States, 2000," CDC: *Morbidity and Mortality Weekly Report* (November 28, 2003), Table 1.
15. Ranjita Misra, "Trends in Abortion Attitudes among Young Adults: 1977–1993," *American Journal of Health Studies* (Spring 2000).
16. Elam-Evans et al., Abstract.
17. "The Abortion Pill," online at www.mayohealth.org
18. Elam-Evans et al.,Table 19.
19. Center for Disease Control, "Maternal Mortality—United States, 1982–1996," *Morbidity and Mortality Weekly Report* (September 4, 1998), 705.
20. E. Hakim-Elahi, H. M. Tovell, and M. S. Burnhill, "Complications of First-Trimester Abortion: A Report of 170,000 Cases," *Obstetrics and*

Gynecology (July 1990), 1145–1146.

21. M. J. Goldacre et al., "Abortion and Breast Cancer: A Case-Control Record Linkage Study," *Journal of Epidemiology and Community Health* (May 2001), p. 336.

22. Wendy J. Lewis, "Factors Associated with Post-Abortion Adjustment Problems: Implications for Triage," *The Canadian Journal of Human Sexuality* (Spring 1997), 9–16.

23. Zhou W. Nielsen, H. Larsen, and J. Olsen, "Induced Abortion and Placenta Complications in the Subsequent Pregnancy," *Acta Obstetrica et Gynecologica Scandinavica* (December 2001), 1115–1120.

24. "Laws and Regulations Affecting Medical Abortion," Center for Reproductive Law and Policy (July 2001) at www.crlp.org

25. B. S. Jones and S. Heller, "Providing Medical Abortion: Legal Issues of Relevance to Providers," *Journal of the American Medical Women's Association* (June 2000), 145–150.

26. J. K. Pearson, "Editorial: Perspectives on Abortion and Population Planning," *Patient Care* (September 30, 1998), p. 7.

27. Bradley Smith, *The American Way of Sex* (New York: Two Continents, 1978), p. 232.

28. I. T. Gaw Gonzalo et al., "Levonorgestrel Implants (Norplant II) for Male Contraception Clinical Trials: Combination with Transdermal and Injectable Testosterone," *Journal of Clinical Endocrinology and Metabolism* (August 2002), 3562–3572

29. D. Ren et al., "A Sperm Ion Channel Required for Sperm Motility and Male Fertility," *Nature* (October 11, 2001), 603–609.

30. M. McKinney, "Hormone Therapy Shows Promise as a Male Contraceptive," Reuters Health (September 16, 2002).

Chapter 4

1. A. L. Nelson, "Menstrual Problems and Common Gynecological Concerns," *Contraceptive Technology*, 17th ed. (New York: Adams Media, 1998), p. 96.

2. R. B. Ness et al., "Effectiveness of Inpatient and Outpatient Treatment Strategies for Women with Pelvic Inflammatory Disease: Results from the Pelvic Inflammatory Disease Evaluation and Clinical Health (PEACH) Randomized Trial," *American Journal of Obstetrics and Gynecology* (May 2001), 929–937.

3. "Pelvic Inflammatory Disease Fact Sheet," National Institute of Allergy and Infectious Disease, National Institutes of Health, July 1998.

4. A. L. Nelson, p. 125.

5. All data in this section from the American Cancer Society, except as separately noted.

6. B. Cady and J. S. Michaelson, "The Life-Sparing Potential of Mammographic Screening," *Cancer* (May 1, 2001), 1699–1703.

7. B. Rockhill et al., "A Prospective Study of Recreational Physical Activity and Breast Cancer Risk," *Archives of Internal Medicine* (1999), 2290–2296.

8. National Cancer Institute.

9. P. Srivastava, "Roles of Heat-Shock Proteins in Innate and Adaptive Immunity," *Nature Reviews Immunology* (March 1, 2001), 185–194.

10. J. L. Tenore, "Ectopic Pregnancy," *American Family Physician* (September

15, 2000), 1080–1088.

11. Data from the March of Dimes Birth Defects Foundation.

12. Ibid.

13. All statistics for this question from the Centers for Disease Control, except as separately noted.

14. C. R. Eure et al., "Risk of Adverse Pregnancy Outcomes in Young Adolescent Parturients in an Inner-City Hospital," *American Journal of Obstetrics and Gynecology* (May 2002), 918–920.

15. Centers for Disease Control, "Maternal Mortality—United States, 1982–1996," *Morbidity and Mortality Weekly Report* (September 4, 1998), 705–707.

16. Aubrey Milunksy, *Your Genetic Destiny* (Cambridge, MA: Perseus Books, 2001), p. 34.

17. Adapted from J. R. Gardella and J. A. Hill, "Environmental Toxins Associated with Recurrent Pregnancy Loss," *Seminars in Reproductive Medicine* (2000), 407–424.

18. March of Dimes estimate.

19. T. R. Weber et al., "Improved Survival in Congenital Diaphragmatic Hernia with Evolving Therapeutic Strategies," *Archives of Surgery* (May 1998), 498–502; A. Okada et al., "Esophageal Atresia in Osaka: A Review of 39 Years' Experience," *Journal of Pediatric Surgery* (November 1997), 1570–1574.

20. *Health, United States, 2003: With Chartbook on Trends in the Health of Americans*, National Center for Health Statistics, DHHS Pub. No. 2003–1232, (September 2003), p. 153.

21. "Trends in Infant Mortality Attributable to Birth Defects—United States, 1980–1995," *Morbidity and Mortality Weekly Report* (September 25, 1998), 773–778.

22. Data from the Spina Bifida Association of America.

23. B. Ritz et al., "Ambient Air Pollution and Risk of Birth Defects in Southern California," *American Journal of Epidemiology* (January 1, 2002), 17–25.

24. NTP–CERHR Expert Panel Report on Di (2-Ethylhexyl) Phthalate, National Toxicology Program, U.S. Department of Health and Human Services (October 2000).

25. "The Effects of Workplace Hazards on Male Reproductive Health," National Institute for Occupational Safety and Health, 1997, available online at www.cdc.gov/niosh/malrepro.html

26. March of Dimes.

27. Ibid.

28. Margaret A. Honein et al., "Impact of Folic Acid Fortification in the U.S. Food Supply on the Occurrence of Neural Tube Defects," *Journal of the American Medical Association* (June 20, 2001), 2981–2986.

29. The Spina Bifida Association of America.

30. For more information, see the Medical Encyclopedia of the National Library of Medicine at www.nlm.nih.gov/medlineplus/encyclopedia.html

31. Eure et al., 2002.

32. March of Dime Birth Defects Foundation, "Predicting Preterm Birth Still Nearly Impossible," January 4, 2002.

33. *Health, United States, 2003*, p. 153.

34. T. Forsen et al., "The Fetal and Childhood Growth of Persons Who Develop Type 2 Diabetes," *Annals of Internal Medicine* (August 2000), 177.

35. E. Lurbe et al., "Birth Weight Influences Blood Pressure Values and Variability in Children and Adolescents," *Hypertension* (September 2001), p. 389.

36. Barbara Jefferis, C. Power, and C. Hertzman, "Birth Weight, Childhood Socioeconomic Environment, and Cognitive Development in the 1958 British Birth Cohort Study," *British Medical Journal* (August 10, 2002), p. 305.

37. "Low Birth Weight More Likely to Have High Blood Pressure," press release from the American Heart Association, October 20, 2000.

38. Bao-Ping Zhu et al., "Effect of the Interval between Pregnancies on Perinatal Outcomes,"*New England Journal of Medicine* (February 25, 1999), 589–594.

39. Vidya Setty-Venugopal and Ushma D. Upadhyay, *Birth Spacing: Three to Five Saves Lives.* Johns Hopkins Bloomberg School of Public Health: Center for Communication Programs, Population Reports, 2002.

40. Milunsky, p. 90.

41. Ibid.

42. National Institutes of Health, "Sickle Cell Anemia," NIH publication No. 96-4056, November 1996.

43. American Academy of Pediatrics Policy Statement, "Health Support for Children with Marfan Syndrome (RE9639)," November 1996.

44. Bernice Wuethrich, "Why Sex? Putting Theory to the Test," *Science* (September 25, 1998), 1982.

45. Milunsky, p. 34.

46. Q. Yang, S. A. Rasmussen, and J. M. Friedman, "Mortality Associated with Down's Syndrome in the U.S.A. from 1983 to 1997: A Population-Based Study," *Lancet* (March 23, 2002), 1019–1025.

47. Eleanor Mayfield, "New Hope for People with Sickle Cell Anemia," FDA Consumer (May 1996, updated February 1999), available online at www.fda.gov

48. Victor A. McKusick, *Mendelian Inheritance in Man: A Catalog of Human Genes and Genetic Disorders*, 12th ed., (Baltimore: Johns Hopkins University Press, 1998).

Chapter 5

1. "Assisted Reproductive Technology in the United States: 2000 Results Generated from the American Society for Reproductive Medicine/Society for Assisted Reproductive Technology Registry," *Fertility and Sterility* (May 2004), pp. 1207–1220.

2. From E. E. Christensen, T. S. Curry, and J. E. Dowdey, *Introduction to the Physics of Diagnostic Radiology,* 2nd ed. (Philadelphia: Lea & Febeger, 1978), Chapter 25.

3. "Prenatal Care and Tests: Ultrasound in Pregnancy: What Can It Tell You?" May 29, 2001, at www.MayoClinic.com

4. S. C. Blackwell et al., "Five-Year Experience with Midtrimester Amniocentesis Performed by a Single Group of Obstetricians-Gynecologists at a Community Hospital," *American Journal of Obstetrics and Gynecology* (June 2002), 1130–1132.

5. Centers for Disease Control and Prevention, 2001, *Assisted Reproductive Technology Success Rates: National Summary and Fertility Clinic Reports,* CDC: (2003), p. 3.

6. Daniel Dumesic, "Reproductive Health: Male Infertility: Causes and Remedies," November 27, 2000, Mayo Clinic at www.mayoclinic.com.

7. American Society for Reproductive Medicine, "Patient's Fact Sheet:

Diagnostic Testing for Male Factor Infertility," August 2001.

8. "Don't Turn to Assisted Reproduction Too Quickly Warns U.S. Expert," Press release, National Institute of Environmental Health Sciences, July 3, 2002.

9. American Society for Reproductive Medicine, "Fact Sheet: Preimplantation Genetic Diagnosis," December 1996.

10. Y. Verlinsky et al., "Preimplantation Diagnosis for Early-Onset Alzheimer Disease Caused by V717L Mutation," *Journal of the American Medical Association* (February 27, 2002), 1018–1021.

11. Dena Towner and Roberta Springer Loewy, "Ethics of Preimplantation Diagnosis for a Woman Destined to Develop Early-Onset Alzheimer Disease," *Journal of the American Medical Association* (February 27, 2002), 1038–1040.

12. L. A. Shieve et al., "Low and Very Low Birth Weight in Infants Conceived with the Use of Assisted Reproductive Technology," *New England Journal of Medicine* (March 7, 2002), 731–737.

13. M. A. Rossing et al., "Ovarian Tumors in a Cohort of Infertile Women," *New England Journal of Medicine* (September 22, 1994), 771–776.

14. "Patient Fact Sheet: Selective Estrogen Receptor Modulators (SERMs)," American Society for Reproductive Medicine, August 2001.

15. J. L. Simpson and D. J. Lamb, "Genetic Effects of Intracytoplasmic Sperm Injection," *Seminars in Reproductive Medicine* (2001), 239–249.

16. J. L. Simpson, "Are Anomalies Increased after ART and ICSI?" in R.D. Kempers et al., eds, *Fertility and Reproductive Medicine*, Proceedings of the XVI World Congress on Fertility and Sterility, San Francisco (Amsterdam: Elsevier Science, 1998), 199–209.

17. I. Anteby et al., "Ocular Manifestations in Children Born after in Vitro Fertilization," *Archives of Ophthalmology* (October 2001), 1525–1529.

18. K. Pezeshki et al., "Bleeding and Spontaneous Abortion after Therapy for Infertility," *Fertility and Sterility* (September 2000), 504–508.

19. Jong-Hoon Kim et al., "Dopamine Neurons Derived from Embryonic Stem Cells Function in an Animal Model of Parkinson's Disease," *Nature* (July 4, 2002), 50–56.

20. Aileen Constans, "Stem Cell Potential Grows," *The Scientist* (September 2, 2002).

21. D. S. Krause et al., "Multi-Organ, Multi-Lineage Engraftment by a Single Bone Marrow-Derived Stem Cell," *Cell* (May 4, 2001), 369–377.

22. C. Verfaillie et al., "Multipotent Adult Progenitor Cells from Bone Marrow Differentiate into Functional Hepatocyte-like Cells," *Journal of Clinical Investigation* (May 15, 2002), 1291–1302

23. D. Simper et al., "Smooth Muscle Progenitor Cells in Human Blood," *Circulation* (September 3, 2002), 1199–1204.

24. "Stem Cell Transplant Offers Hope to Children with Severe Sickle Cell Disease," American Society of Hematology, Press release, December 6, 2002.

25. "Adult Stem Cells in Orthopaedic Surgery Currently Producing Positive Results," American Academy of Orthopaedic Surgeons, Press release,

October 17, 2002.

26. American Academy of Pediatrics, Work Group on Cord Blood Banking, "Cord Blood Banking for Potential Future Transplantation: Subject Review (RE9860)" (July 1999), 116–118.

27. Rachel Nowak, "Decision Time: A Single Protein May Be the First Step to Customizing Human Stem Cells," *New Scientist* (April 8, 2000).

28. "FAQs About Cloning, Stem Cell Research, and ASRM's Position" at www.asrm.org

29. Coalition for the Advancement of Medical Research, Press release, April 24, 2002.

30. H. Taylor and R. Leitman, "Health Care News," Harris Interactive (June 18, 2001), p. 1.

31. "FASEB Statement of Human Cloning and Human Cloning Legislation," Federation of American Societies for Experimental Biology, July 19, 2001.

32. M. Johnson et al., "Fetal Myelomeningocele (MMC) Repair: Short Term Outcomes," *American Journal of Obstetrics and Gynecology* (December 2001, part 2), S78.

33. N. S. Adzick et al., "Fetal Lung Lesions: Management and Outcomes," *American Journal of Obstetrics and Gynecology* (October 1998), 884–889.

34. A. W. Flake et al., "Treatment of X-Linked Severe Combined Immunodeficiency by in Utero Transplantation of Paternal Bone Marrow," *New England Journal of Medicine* (December 12, 1996), 1806–1810.

35. M. I. Evans et al., "Fetal Therapy," in Aubrey Milunsky ed., *Genetic Disorders and the Fetus, Diagnosis, Prevention, and Treatment*, 4th ed., (Baltimore: Johns Hopkins University Press, 1998), 968.

36. "Researchers Refine Technique for in Utero Correction of the Genetic Defect Associated with Cystic Fibrosis," News from the 2001 Clinical Congress, American College of Surgeons (October 7–12, 2001).

GLOSSARY

Abortion. Termination of a pregnancy. See *Induced abortion* and *Miscarriage.*

Afterbirth. The placenta and other membranes expelled from the uterus after childbirth.

Alpha-fetoprotein. A protein made in the fetus, which may be measured in the mother's blood and in the amniotic fluid.

Amniocentesis. The microscopic and biochemical examination of embryonic cells and amniotic fluid to diagnose genetic or developmental abnormalities.

Amniotic fluid. The liquid that surrounds the fetus, contained within the membrane, the amnion. Commonly called the "bag of waters."

Antibody. A protein made by the immune system that attacks foreign proteins and disease-causing organisms.

Assisted reproductive technology (ART). A medical or surgical procedure carried out to achieve pregnancy.

Birth defect. A medical problem present at birth.

Blastocyst. An embryo in early stages of cell division immediately following fertilization.

Breast. The mammary gland of human females that produces milk after childbirth.

Breech birth. The emergence of a baby's buttocks or feet first through the birth canal.

Cervical cap. A birth-control device similar to a diaphragm, but smaller, that fits over the cervix and stops sperm from entering.

Cervix. The lower end of the uterus at the top of the vagina.

Cesarean (cesarean section or C-section). Surgical delivery of a fetus through incisions in the abdomen and uterus.

Chorionic villi. Fingerlike projections of the chorion filled with fetal blood vessels that extend into the lining of the uterus and form the fetal part of the placenta.

Chorionic villus sampling. A medical screening test (usually done between 10 and 12 weeks of pregnancy) in which cells taken from the chorionic villi are examined for abnormal chromosomes and other signs of birth defects.

Chromosome. A dark-staining body that becomes visible in the nucleus of a cell during cell division. Each chromosome contains a single molecule of the genetic material, DNA. See also *Gene.*

Clone. A genetic duplicate of a cell or a whole organism produced from the genetic material in a body cell.

Condom. A sheath of latex or plastic placed

over the penis (in males) or inside the vagina (in females) to prevent pregnancy and disease transmission.

Contraceptive. Any drug or device used to prevent pregnancy.

Contraction. The shortening and thickening of a muscle. Specifically, the strong, rhythmic, squeezing motion of the uterus during labor.

Corpus luteum. A yellow endocrine gland in the ovary. It develops from a ruptured follicle soon after an egg is released.

Cytoplasm. All the material in a cell except the nucleus.

Diaphragm. A cap placed over the cervix to prevent sperm from entering the uterus.

Dilation. The widening of the cervix during labor or during a medical procedure.

Dilation and curettage (D&C). A medical procedure in which the contents of the uterus are scraped or suctioned out. Used as a treatment for uterine disorders and for some elective abortions before week 14.

DNA. The molecule in the nucleus of cells that controls development and inheritance of characteristics. A gene is a piece of DNA.

Doppler ultrasound. A procedure that uses the change of frequency of sound waves to measure rates of blood flow, etc.

Down syndrome. A birth defect characterized by heart defects and mental retardation and caused by an extra chromosome 21 (or a piece of it).

Dystocia. The slowing or stopping of labor.

Eclampsia. Seizures occurring in a pregnant woman resulting from preeclampsia. See *Preeclampsia.*

Ectoderm. The outermost of the three cell layers in an embryo, which develops into skin and the nervous system.

Ectopic pregnancy. The implantation of a zygote outside the uterus, usually in a fallopian tube.

Egg. A reproductive cell produced by the ovary of a female.

Ejaculation. The ejection of semen from the penis.

Embryo. An unborn human between fertilization and 10 weeks of pregnancy.

Endoderm. The innermost of the three cell layers of an embryo, which develops into the internal organs of the digestive, respiratory, and excretory systems.

Epididymis. A mass of coiled ducts in which sperm mature after their manufacture in the seminiferous tubules.

Estrogen. A female hormone, produced in the ovaries, that regulates the menstrual cycle and performs many other functions. See also *Progesterone.*

Fallopian tube. Either of the two outbranches of the uterus that accepts eggs from the ovaries.

Fertilization. Union of sperm and egg.

Fetal alcohol syndrome. Physical and mental birth defects caused by a woman drinking alcohol during pregnancy.

Fetal distress. A threat to the life of the fetus, usually a lack of oxygen during labor or delivery.

Fetus. An unborn human between ten weeks of pregnancy and birth.

Folic acid. One of the B vitamins; adequate intake reduces risk of neural tube defects.

Follicle. An egg-containing cluster of cells in the ovary.

Follicle stimulating hormone (FSH). A hormone made in the pituitary gland that stimulates the development of ovarian follicles in females and the production of sperm in males.

Full-term. Birth after 37 weeks of pregnancy.

Gene. The basic hereditary unit. A segment of a DNA molecule in a chromosome.

Genetic counseling. Information provided to parents regarding risks, testing, and treatment for inherited disorders or birth defects.

Genetic disorder. Any inherited disease, including chromosomal disorders and gene mutations.

Gonadotropin. Any hormone that regulates the functions of the sex organs.

Gonadotropin-releasing hormone (GnRH). A hormone secreted by the hypothalamus that stimulates the release of gonadotropins (FSH and LH) by the pituitary gland.

Hormone. A chemical secretion of one organ that affects another organ.

Human chorionic gonadotropin (hCG). A hormone made in the placenta during pregnancy that triggers the release of estrogen and progesterone from the ovary.

Implantation. The attachment of the blastocyst to the lining of the uterus about one week after fertilization.

Induced abortion. The intentional termination of a pregnancy, using a surgical procedure or drugs.

Infertility. In women, the inability to become pregnant or to maintain a pregnancy to full-term by ordinary means; in men the inability to impregnate a woman through sexual intercourse.

Intracytoplasmic sperm injection (ICSI). A procedure to treat infertility in which a sperm is injected into an egg.

In vitro fertilization (IVF). A procedure to treat infertility, in which egg and sperm are combined outside the body and two or more of the resulting embryos are introduced into the uterus for implantation.

Labor. The process of childbirth, in which the rhythmic contractions of the uterine muscles open the cervix and push the fetus through the birth canal.

Laparoscopy. A surgical procedure in which internal organs are viewed through an incision in the abdominal wall, using a thin, lighted microscope.

Low birth weight. An infant weight of less than 2,500 grams at birth.

Luteinizing hormone (LH). A hormone made and released by the pituitary gland that stimulates egg release in females and testosterone production in males.

Mammary gland. Milk-producing gland; breast.

Mammogram. An X-ray examination of the breasts used to detect breast cancer.

Menstrual cycle. The (approximately) 28-day cycle of growth and shedding of the lining of the uterus if there is no pregnancy.

Mesoderm. The middle one of the three main cell layers in the embryo, which becomes connective tissues, bones, muscles, blood, and blood vessels.

Miscarriage. The unintended expulsion of embryo or fetus from the uterus before 20 weeks. Spontaneous abortion.

Mucus. Any thick fluid secretion from a gland or membrane.

Multiple birth. More than one baby born as the result of a single pregnancy.

Neural Tube Defect (NTD). Any one of several abnormalities of the brain and spinal cord that develop as a result of failure of the neural tube to close in the early embryo.

Nucleus. The dense body inside a cell that contains DNA.

Ovary. The female reproductive organ that releases eggs.

Ovulation. The (approximately) monthly release of an egg from an ovary.

Oxytocin. A hormone with several functions, including causing the uterus to contract during labor.

Pap smear. A microscopic examination of cells to detect cancer of the cervix.

Pelvic inflammatory disease (PID). A bacterial infection in any of the female reproductive organs.

Penis. The external male organ through

which urine and semen leave the body.

Pituitary. A gland at the base of the brain that produces sex hormones (among others).

Placenta. The flat, round organ in the uterus during pregnancy that exchanges food, oxygen, and waste products between woman and fetus.

Pregnancy. In human females, the condition of a fertilized egg attached to the uterus and the period a developing embryo/fetus is carried in the uterus.

Preterm. Birth before 37 weeks of pregnancy.

Progesterone. A hormone made and released mostly by the corpus luteum. After implantation, it maintains the uterine lining and prepares the breasts to secrete milk.

Prostaglandins. A category of hormones with many functions, including inducing labor.

Prostate gland. In the male, one of the three glands that secrete the fluid portion of semen.

Puberty. The process of reaching sexual maturity, usually occurring between ages 11 and 19.

Scrotum. The skin-covered pouch that contains the testicles.

Semen. Sperm and liquid discharged by a male during ejaculation.

Sex chromosome. A chromosome that determines the gender of an individual.

Sexual intercourse. The insertion of the male penis into the female vagina.

Sexual reproduction. The production of offspring from two specialized cells: a male sex cell, or sperm; and a female sex cell, or egg.

Sexually transmitted disease (STD). A disease passed from one person to another during sexual contact.

Sonogram. See *Ultrasound scan.*

Sperm. Male reproductive cells produced in the testicles.

Spermicide. A contraceptive chemical introduced into a woman's vagina that prevents pregnancy by killing sperm.

Spina bifida. A neural tube defect in which some part of the spinal cord is exposed in an infant.

Spontaneous abortion. See *Miscarriage.*

Sterility. Permanent and total inability to reproduce.

Testicles. The male reproductive organs, lying inside the scrotum, that produce sperm.

Testosterone. The primary sex hormone in males.

Tubal ligation. A sterilization procedure in which a woman's fallopian tubes are cut or tied off.

Ultrasound scan. A procedure that uses high-frequency sound waves to produce images of internal organs.

Umbilical cord. The ropelike structure that connects the fetus to the placenta.

Uterus. The pear-shaped organ in which an embryo/fetus develops.

Vagina. The muscular tube lying between the uterus and the external genitals of a female.

Vas deferens. The tube that carries sperm from the epididymis to the penis.

Vasectomy. A surgical procedure in which a man's vas deferens is cut, preventing sperm from being ejaculated.

Very low birth weight. A weight of less than 1,500 grams at birth.

Zygote. A fertilized egg.

FOR FURTHER INFORMATION

Books

Avraham, Regina. *The Reproductive System.* Philadelphia: Chelsea House, 2001.

Connell, Elizabeth. *The Contraception Sourcebook.* New York: McGraw-Hill/Contemporary Books, 2001.

Curtis, Glade B., and Judith Schuler. *Your Pregnancy Week by Week*, 5th ed. Cambridge, MA: Perseus Books, 2004.

Davis, Elizabeth. *Heart & Hands: A Midwife's Guide to Pregnancy and Birth*, 4th ed. Berkeley, CA: Celestial Arts, 2004.

Knowles, Jon, and Marcia Ringel. *All About Birth Control: A Personal Guide.* New York: Three Rivers Press/Crown, 1998.

Milunksy, Aubrey. *Your Genetic Destiny: Know Your Genes, Secure Your Health, and Save Your Life.* Cambridge, MA: Perseus, 2001.

Murkoff, Heidi, Arlene Eisenberg, and Sandra Hathaway. *What to Expect When You're Expecting*, 3rd ed. New York: Workman, 2002.

Nathanielsz, Peter W. *Life in the Womb: The Origin of Health and Disease.* Ithaca, NY: Promethean Press, 1999.

Scientific American. *Understanding Cloning.* New York: Warner, 2002.

————. *Understanding the Genome.* New York: Warner, 2002.

Sears, William, and Martha Sears. *The Pregnancy Book: Month-by-Month, Everything You Need to Know from America's Baby Experts.* New York: Little, Brown, 1997.

Stoppard, Miriam. *Conception, Pregnancy, and Birth.* New York: Dorling Kindersley, 2000.

Vaughan, Christopher. *How Life Begins: The Science of Life in the Womb.* New York: Delta, 1996.

Articles

Almasi, Mary Rose. "A Smarter, Healthier Pregnancy." *Child* (March 2002), p. 67+.

Avery, Sarah. "A Chance for Anna." (Fetal surgery.) *Reader's Digest* (July 2003), pp. 84–90.

Backer, Rachel. "What It's Like to Be Pregnant." *Cosmopolitan* (July 2004), p. 138+.

Begley, Sharon. "Shaped by Life in the Womb." *Newsweek* (April 27, 1999), pp. 50–57.

Christensen, Damaris. "Male Choice: The Search for a New Contraceptive for Men." *Science News* (September 30, 2000), p. 222.

Cicero, Karen. "The Inside Guide to Prenatal Testing." *Parents Magazine* (January 2002), pp. 106–108.

Glatzer, Randi. "Surprise! Half of All Pregnancies Are Accidents." *Self* (May 2003), p. 194+.

Gorman, Christine. "Born Too Soon." *Time* (October 18, 2004), p.73.

James-Enger, Kelly. "Does Your Birth Control Fit Your Lifestyle?" *Parents Magazine* (May 2001), pp. 75+.

McGinnis, Marianne. "Baby's Cord Blood: Should You Bank It?" *Prevention* (May 2004), p. 137.

Meadows, Michele. "Pregnancy and the Drug Dilemma." *FDA Consumer* (May 2001), p. 26.

Mulrine, Anna. "Making Babies." (Assisted reproductive technology.) *U. S. News & World Report* (September 27, 2004), pp. 60–69.

Shawn, Gina. "My Battle with Breast Cancer." *Redbook* (September 2004), pp. 164+.

On the Internet

www.innerbody.com. Study the anatomy of the human body, including the male and female reproductive systems, at this award-winning site.

www.med.utah.edu/andrology/photo_gallery .html. The University of Utah's photo gallery of sperm cells.

www.stanford.edu/group/Urchin/sperm-l.htm. Watch a sperm swim, courtesy of Stanford University. See www.stanford.edu/group/Urchin/nos.htm for a computer animation of the chemical events that occur at fertilization.

embryo.soad.umich.edu. The Multidimensional Human Embryo project shows magnetic resonance imaging (MRI), rotational, and animations of development from fertilization to 10 weeks of pregnancy.

www.firstvisit.org allows you to customize a simulation of what your visit with an obstetrician/gynecologist will be like.

www.americanbaby.com has a message board and columns written by experts on all aspects of pregnancy and parenting.

www.otispregnancy.org for information on the effects of drugs taken during pregnancy or to find a Teratology Information Service center in your state. Or call the toll-free hotline at 1-888-285-3410.

www.parents.com. *Parents* magazine maintains a full set of resources and practical advice on pregnancy and childbirth.

Agencies and Organizations

Advocates for Youth
Suite 200
1025 Vermont Avenue NW
Washington, D.C. 20005
www.advocatesforyouth.org
Request pamphlets "Advice from Teens on Buying Condoms" and "Your Guide to the Clinic."

American Academy of Pediatrics
141 Northwest Point Boulevard
Elk Grove Village, IL 60007
www.aap.org
Publishes books on parenting and child care.

American Cancer Society
P.O. Box 102454
Atlanta, GA 30326
www.cancer.org
Local chapters and offices in many communities.

American College of Nurse-Midwives
818 Connecticut Avenue NW, Suite 900
Washington, D.C. 20006
www.acnm.org
Ask for information on a career as a certified nurse midwife.

American College of Obstetricians and Gynecologists
409 12th Street SW
Washington, D.C. 20090
www.acog.org
Publishes "You and Your Sexuality" and "Your First Ob-Gyn Visit."

American Sickle Cell Anemia Association
10300 Carnegie Avenue
Cleveland, OH 44106
www.ascaa.org
Promotes care, counseling, testing services, and awareness of sickle cell anemia.

American Society for Reproductive Medicine
1209 Montgomery Highway
Birmingham, Alabama 35216
www.asrm.org
Offers patient fact sheets on in vitro fertilization, genetic screening, and birth defects.

Association of Reproductive Health Professionals
2401 Pennsylvania Avenue NW, Suite 350
Washington, D.C. 20037
www.arhp.org
Request the pamphlets "Birth Control: Comparing the Choices" and "Today and Every Day: Contraceptive Confidence" in either English or Spanish.

Cystic Fibrosis Foundation
6931 Arlington Road
Bethesda, Maryland 20814
www.cff.org
Publishes "An Introduction to Cystic
Fibrosis for Patients and Families."

Family Health International
P.O. Box 13950
Research Triangle Park, NC 27709
www.fhi.org
Distributes information on family planning
and women's health in 40 countries.

Genetics and Birth Defects Alliance of
Genetic Support Groups
4301 Connecticut Avenue NW, Suite 404
Washington, D.C. 20008
www.geneticalliance.org
A consortium of support groups for specific
genetic disorders.

International Council on Infertility
P.O. Box 6836
Arlington, VA 22206
www.inciid.org
Publishes fact sheets and a newsletter on
infertility, adoption, and parenting.

Kaiser Family Foundation
2400 Sand Hill Road
Menlo Park, CA 94015
www.kff.org
Check out the SexSmarts Web site, a part-
nership with *Seventeen* magazine.

March of Dimes Birth Defects Foundation
1275 Mamaroneck Avenue
White Plains, NY 10605
www.modimes.org
Provides information on birth defects and
refers individuals to local counseling services.

Maternal and Child Health Bureau
18-05 Parklawn Building
5600 Fishers Lane
Rockville, MD 20857
www.ask.hrsa.gov/MCH.cfm
Search the Bureau's clearinghouse on any
topic related to reproduction and health.

National Abortion Federation
1755 Massachusetts Avenue NW, Suite 600
Washington, D.C. 20036
www.prochoice.org
The professional association of abortion
providers.

National Campaign to Prevent Teen
Pregnancy
2100 M Street NW, Suite 300
Washington D.C. 20037
www.teenpregnancy.org
Take the weekly survey on their Web site
and learn how to avoid pregnancy.

National Cancer Institute
Office of Cancer Communications
Building 31, Room 10A-03
31 Center Drive
Bethesda, MD 20892
www.nci.nih.gov
Order free publications online on any
cancer-related topic.

National Right to Life Committee
512 10th Street NW
Washington, D.C. 20004
www.nrlc.org
The nation's best-known anti-abortion
activist group.

National Tay-Sachs and Allied Diseases
Association
2001 Beacon Street, Suite 204
Brighton, MA 02135
www.ntsad.org
Publishes pamphlets on Tay-Sachs,
Canavan, and related diseases.

National Women's Health Network
514 10th Street NW, Suite 400
Washington, D.C. 20004
www.womenshealthnetwork.org
Publishes pamphlets on a wide range of topics related to women's health.

Planned Parenthood Federation of America
810 Seventh Avenue
New York, NY 10019
www.plannedparenthood.org
The best source of information, contraception, and emergency services for teens and
young adults. Call 1-800-230-PLAN or
check the phone book for a local clinic.

RESOLVE: National Fertility Association
1310 Broadway
Somerville, MA 02144
www.resolve.org
Maintains local chapters and publishes a
newsletter.

Sickle Cell Disease Association of America
200 Corporate Pointe, Suite 495
Culver City, California 90230
sicklecelldisease.org
An advocacy group for sickle-cell research.

Society for Adolescent Medicine
1916 NW Copper Oaks Circle
Blue Springs, MO 64015
www.adolescenthealth.org
The society helps teens find a physician in
their area who specializes in health care for
people ages 12–21.

Spina Bifida Association of America
4590 MacArthur Boulevard NW, Suite 250
Washington, D.C. 20007
www.sbaa.org
Local chapters provide information on neural tube defects and assistance to parents of
children with spina bifida.

United Mitochondrial Diseases Foundation
P.O. Box 1151
Monroeville, PA 15146
www.umdf.org
Publishes the newsletter "Mitochondrial
News."

INDEX